M000158304

THE ULTIMATE
GREENVILLE
RELOCATION
GUIDE

♡ Greenville

Libby McMillan Henson

The Ultimate Greenville Relocation Guide
First Edition

Table of Contents

Greenville: A Great Move!

If you've decided to move to Greenville—or circumstances have brought you here—lucky you! Greenville will afford you a truly *wonderful* quality of life. Greenville's amazing downtown likely made one heck of a first impression, and you've probably discovered how incredibly nice the people are, too. This area also offers more fun and more natural beauty than you can squeeze into a lifetime of trying to see and do it all.

Greenville's Falls, as seen from The Liberty Bridge
Photo courtesy of D.J. Henson

If you *haven't* yet decided, but the concept has come up in conversation (or even daydreams), just keep reading. Most of the tools you need, to make your decision, or to dive into a happy new life, are included within these pages. This beautiful city has her arms wide open for you.

10 Reasons Why You'll Love Living in Greenville

Reason #1: Friendly People

Greenville, South Carolina is one of the friendliest cities in the USA, a place where strangers make eye contact, smile openly and offer up a friendly greeting to anyone within earshot. Guys of all ages hold open doors for the gals, and

1

drivers allow waiting cars to get out into the flow. Locals are genuinely caring and interested in others. A generosity of spirit is quickly evident here, a factor which goes a long way in feeling at home. All the pluses of Southern civility are alive and well in this bustling small city.

Reason #2: A Strong Economy & Innovative Spirit

Sited halfway between Charlotte and Atlanta—in what the international business community calls the "Charlanta megaregion"—Greenville has a strong economy and has positioned itself for a very bright future. More than 240 international businesses call the area home; our Inland Port gives international concerns another great reason to join the forty Fortune 500 companies which were already here as of early 2016. Greenville is focused on innovation, from its schools and public/private partnerships to the many incubators and high-tech industries flourishing here. The past is respected, but Greenville looks forward; officials and influencers are strategically moving toward the future they create.

Nearby Caesars Head is a favorite day trip
Photo courtesy of D.J. Henson

Reason #3: One Hour to the Mountains, Three Hours to the Beach

Not many places in America can claim that dual proximity, but Greenville can! Situated in the rolling foothills of the Blue Ridge Mountains, your new

2

city is just an hour from countless waterfalls, hiking trails, ziplines and scenic overlooks (including the Blue Ridge Parkway). Dupont State Forest, Jones Gap, Lake Jocassee, Table Rock State Park and other glorious attractions are all an easy drive from Greenville. We even have our own mountain destination right in town: Paris Mountain State Park.

But any weekend you decide you need a little sand in between your toes, you can be on a beautiful beach in just about three hours. And there are so many gorgeous places within an hour of Greenville, your biggest problem will be choosing that day's adventure. It's a great problem to have, trying to decide what to go experience in a place this beautiful.

Reason #4: Cost of Living

Greenville's annual cost of living has, in recent years, remained a few points below the national average. The Greenville Area Development Council (GADC) website has the latest stats, and a handy cost-of-living calculator to compare your current or former city to here. There's a good chance your money will go further here!

Reason #5: Diversity

Some get a pleasant surprise they don't anticipate: diversity is simply a way of life here. You can certainly put aside any race-based concerns you may have about living in the South or about Greenville. It's a wonderfully accepting and supportive place; its multi-cultural festivals and the social interaction of locals quickly bear this out.

Greenville's business environment also plays a role in the many cultures found here. "The international community here is disproportionately large because of BMW and Michelin," explains Mayor Knox White, who has helped his city grow from sleepy textile town to internationally renowned hub for automotive engineering, research, logistics, tech and life sciences. "You'll hear German, French, Indian, Chinese, lots of foreign languages," says the mayor. "People also experience a lot of foreign language on a *flight* to Greenville," he adds with a knowing smile, "and it catches them off guard."

3

Greenville's lush Main Street hosts Saturday's TD Market
Photo courtesy of D.J. Henson

Reason #6: An Amazing Downtown

Newcomers are flocking to Greenville's vibrant urban center to live. It's also a fantastic place to just hang out. Jaw-dropping waterfalls beneath a beautiful suspension bridge and the most beautiful park you've ever seen...free concerts three nights a week...brownstones, loft apartments, and ballpark condos...a dazzling variety of restaurants, theaters, galleries and bars...a lush green canopy over Main Street...a university presence...a popular farmers market...and a bike trail running right through it all. What more could you want in a downtown? Imagine bringing your own friends to the Liberty Bridge and watching their stunned reaction...

Reason #7: Weather & Seasons

Winter is short and never brutal. Snow days happen so rarely, they are exciting (but short-lived). Spring is like something out of a dream, when the entire county bursts into pink, white, yellow and purple blossoms. Summer is comfortable at our higher elevations and Greenville life is all about the outdoors. Fall is spectacular. The best way to spend a glorious autumn day is by driving a back road toward a favorite mountain overlook. You'll soon have your own favorite.

4

Reason #8: Entertainment & Cultural Opportunities

The city's cultural offerings are world-class and surprisingly abundant, given its size. You can enjoy world-class touring acts, Broadway shows, cutting-edge theater, dance, and a renowned symphony, all right in your own downtown. The city's annual Euphoria food wine & music festival is a must for your calendar, and live music is plentiful across the area. There's no shortage of sports to play or watch: The Greenville Drive minor league team feeds the Red Sox, while fans of The Swamp Rabbits hockey team say "Fear the Ears!" Gallery walks, museum events and philanthropic galas round out the list of ways you can while away your free time.

Reason #9: Water, Water Everywhere

The focal point is always water in Greenville—notice the city's logo, in which the 'g' forms a river—and that's because of the Reedy River and its amazing waterfalls. The Falls and downtown's other water features also remind residents of the countless natural treasures within easy reach. These include internationally acclaimed Lake Jocassee, beautiful Lake Keowee, the French Broad and wild Chattooga Rivers. From serene mountain lakes to some of the world's best whitewater, you can boat, paddle, stand up paddle (SUP), fish or just enjoy a stellar water view, including—if you choose—from home.

Reason #10: Bragging Rights

The national awards that Greenville's won in the past few years fill residents with a sense of regional pride, a pride you'll share the moment you make the decision to move here. If the decision was made for you, you just hit the jackpot!

Best Places to Live 2016	Men's Journal
#2 Best Town Ever	Outside Magazine
#3 Best Downtown in America, 2016	Livability
Best in the US, 2015	Lonely Planet
US Metro Areas with the Most Pride	Gallup
Top 10 Best Parks in U.S.	Trip Advisor
Top Six Hot Spots for Travel in the World	CBS This Morning
Best Al Fresco Dining Neighborhoods	USA TODAY 10Best

5

Best Urban Trails	USA TODAY 10Best
Best Urban Bike Paths	Fodor's
Top 10 US Park	Trip Advisor
#14 of 14,000 America's Best Downtowns	Forbes
Top 10 Cycling Cities in the United States	Global Cycling Network
The South's Best Farmers' Markets	Southern Living
This Year's Great Southern Food Destination	Southern Living
America's Best Main Streets	Parade magazine
Top 10 Small Cities Where Biz Thrives	Entrepreneur
Top 10 Best Downtowns	Livability.com
Top 10 Places You Have to Visit	MSN Travel
The South's Tastiest Towns	Southern Living
Micro City of the Future (#1)	fDi Intelligence
Emerging Biotech Hubs	Business Facilities

If you like hosting out-of-town friends, make sure your guest room is comfy. Once someone experiences Greenville for the first time, he or she is highly likely to come back…and back…and back again. Greenville mesmerizes all who visit her.

Hot Tip: Keep a copy of this book in your own guest room. It helps you tell the story of your new city!

Other resources will also be helpful as you explore your options, including the amazing VisitGreenvilleSC bureau and welcome center; friendly and insightful local tour guides; our many comfortable hotels; and local blogs and websites.

Note from the Author

I had the dream of moving here the first time I saw the Falls. It was the gorgeous Hubbell building out on I-85 which had drawn me into the city. I headed downtown and got the surprise of my life.

Like you, I'm sure, it was love at first sight. Falls Park and Liberty Bridge were about the prettiest things I'd ever seen in an American city. Having lived in flat Florida for 20 years, I was also thrilled by Greenville's rolling topography, the height of its trees and the vivid hues of its lush flora. I loved the Furman campus, the 'wow' factor of the CU-ICAR buildings and the welcoming facades of all the Craftsman cottages near downtown. Access to good fried okra and cornbread didn't hurt, either; nor did the city's abundance of avid college football fans.

I came back on assignment, with an architect friend happily in tow. We thoroughly enjoyed our meeting with Mayor Knox White, whose enthusiasm for his own city was (and still is) infectious. His tour of the city made me quickly realize I was truly somewhere special. On my next trip here, it was warm out, and the car adjacent to mine at a stoplight also had its windows down. The locals in the other car caught my eye, smiled and drawled out a friendly "Heyyyyyyyy" while we waited for the light to change. *And that was it.* That was the moment I knew this would be the perfect place to build a new life. And it has been.

Greenville is beautiful inside and out. Read on, and let me help you discover this great place to live.

–Libby

CHAPTER 1:
GETTING ORIENTED AND WHAT TO EXPECT

Geographic Orientation

Where exactly is Greenville? Getting oriented, particularly in a new part of the country, is a fun challenge.

Hot Tip: In the Handy Reference Section at the back of this book, you'll find a critical chart called **Getting Around / Roads To Know,** *designed to help you navigate* **within the greater Greenville area.** *Use it and you'll save <u>countless</u> hours of frustration: learning how to navigate this area is the only tough part about living here!*

Now let's get you oriented. Your new home is in a really convenient location. Greenville essentially lies halfway between Atlanta and Charlotte, on the diagonal line that is I-85. Another way to describe the city's location is that it's an hour south of Asheville, nestled up to the Blue Ridge Mountain foothills. Greenville is also three hours from coastal beaches and equidistant to New York and South Florida. Take a look:

Travel Time from Greenville	Distance in miles	By Car	By Plane
Atlanta	144	2hr 20m	1hr
Charleston, SC	212	3hr 15m	2hr 45m
Charlotte	104	1hr 45m	50m
Chicago	707	11hr 15m	2hr
Cincinnati	415	6hr 40m	3hr 5m
Cleveland	610	9hr 30m	3hr 20m
Jacksonville, FL	389	5hr 45m	3hr 5m
Nashville	346	5hr 40m	3hr 5m
New York	722	11hr 40m	2hr
Raleigh-Durham	263	4hr 15m	2hr 30m
Savannah, GA	259	4hr	2hr 30m
Tampa	598	9hr 5m	3hr 15m
Washington, DC	498	7hr 50m	1hr 25m

9

New York
Chicago
Cleveland
Cincinnati
Washington DC
Raleigh
Charlotte
Nashville
Atlanta
Charleston
Savannah
Jacksonville
Tampa

Fun Fact: Greenville is within 20 miles of two delivery terminals along a major pipeline connecting Louisiana and the mid-Atlantic; our gasoline prices are consistently some of the cheapest in the US.

Even GSP airport is beautiful
Photo courtesy of GreenvilleRelocation.com

Flying to & from Greenville

Prefer to fly? Our great location gives quick access to the entire eastern half of the country. **Washington D.C.** is just over one hour by air; **New York** is only slightly longer. **Fort Lauderdale** is an hour and a half. **Dallas** is a two hour flight. A few direct flights go to major cities from here, but you'll typically connect through Charlotte, Atlanta or another airline hub. As of this writing, all international flights connect through a major metro.

Greenvillians have a lot of airport choices. Greenville-Spartanburg (**GSP**) is small and easy, and is served by all the major airlines and one low-cost carrier. Nearby Asheville (**AVL**) mainly offers connecting flights to Charlotte and Atlanta, but currently gives locals some low-cost options to Florida. Charlotte's Douglas International (**CLT**), however, offers direct flights to 140 cities, including major European metros. Private pilots use Greenville's downtown airport.

Atlanta's Hartsfield-Jackson International Airport (**ATL**) is a bit of a hassle to reach from Greenville, as you have to cross the city to reach its south-side location. Long-term parking can cancel out any flight savings obtained by the drive.

Welcome to "the Upstate"

South Carolina is divided into four regions: the Lowcountry, the Midlands, the Pee Dee (named for a river) and Greenville's area, the beautiful northwestern Upstate, where cooler temps and higher elevations mean lovely summers and gorgeous terrain.

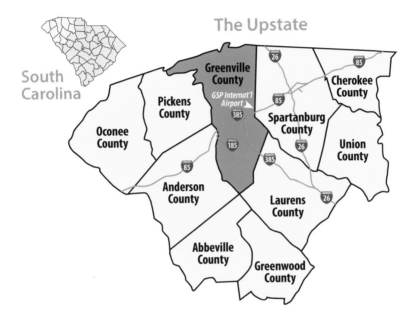

Your New Weekend Destinations

Depending on the season, you'll head into the mountains of western North Carolina or down to the beach…and that's the beauty of Greenville. Believe it or not, there's even snow-skiing within a three hour drive.

Romantic **Charleston** is easily yours for a weekend, with its gracious architecture, mossy oaks, dreamy gardens and delicious food. This southern "lowcountry" city makes for a lovely getaway and is only three hours by car. Beaches near Charleston span the gamut from upscale **Kiawah** and **Isle of Palms** to non-commercial **Edisto** (*ED-is-stow*). It's fun to explore the islands represented by all those black and white oval-shaped stickers you'll see happily displayed on Greenville car windows.

12

A lucky few snare a vacation home in the elite but friendly community atop nearby **Caesars Head** mountain, a place to escape summer heat with only a 45 minute drive. A more typical mountain weekend would be in western North Carolina or north Georgia. Because the Upstate is situated within an **easy drive of four other states** (GA, NC, TN and VA), each offering an array of road-trip opportunities.

Tours & Assistance

For a personal and entertaining macro-view of your new home area, schedule a tour with **Make Greenville Yours.** This company's personal and insightful tours of Greenville County (and sometimes beyond) are a fantastic way to get visually oriented without the hassle of trying to navigate while you're trying to soak it all in. You'll also be learning as you go, while your guide weaves the story of the Upstate, and includes major local landmarks you pass or stop to see. You'll meet new friends during your tour, and come away with a much clearer understanding of your new city. Owner and guide Mike Cruice is a 30-year resident of the area.

Tour guide Mike Cruice of Make Greenville Yours
Photo courtesy of GreenvilleRelocation.com

13

Author John Nolan of **Greenville History Tours** brings downtown to live via his own tours, some of which are on foot. Choose **history or cuisine** as your focus; a BBQ tour is also an option. **Greenville Glides** offers another way to see Greenville, during its two-hour Segway tour of downtown.

Local Culture

No matter where we move, there are always things to learn about a new hometown. Sometimes we're predisposed to thinking a place will be a certain way because of factors like media, literature or regional stereotypes. Greenville is definitely Southern, but has its own ways. Whether you choose to adapt to local traditions, or merely just want a better understanding of what you see and hear, this chapter will be a big help to you.

The People

A large part of the local population grew up here and stayed. Even before downtown was wonderful, the Greenville area had friendly people, good weather and amazing natural beauty. Now more so than ever, the city's popularity and media attention are spurring young adults who grow up here to return quickly after college.

Places like The Gorge in nearby Saluda, NC appeal to active families
Photo courtesy of Karin Strickland for The Gorge

14

The area's focus on automotive engineering, tech, life sciences and logistics, however, also brings in all sorts of fascinating internationals in as part of the workforce. And a higher-than-normal percentage of area residents are engineers, due to Fluor, BMW, GE Energy and Michelin being here.

You'll find a burgeoning creative class as well as outfitters, realtors, investment bankers and other professionals. The area's natural beauty appeals to folks from all walks of life, while the progressive nature of the Upstate, and the national press it receives, are magnets for interesting people.

Graciousness and Civility

Congratulations, you've just chosen the friendliest city ever for your new home. Expect lots of casual greetings—from total strangers—in the form of a honey-coated "heyyyyy."

Manners are more than important in Greenville; they're a way of life. Young boys call women "ma'am" and mean it as a sign of courtesy and respect. Doors are held open for females. Single guys in their twenties write and mail thank-you notes. (Buy a box as soon as possible; sending one to repay a kindness or acknowledge a hosted event will make a terrific early impression on new local friends).

Kindness, courtesy and the benefit of a doubt are the rule, not the exception. Need to make a left turn? Don't worry, it won't be difficult…because someone will let you out. Need a helping hand with something heavy? It could easily appear, as if by magic. And if it doesn't, it's perfectly fine to say "Hey, y'all, could you please help me for a second?"

The Look

Greenville has a conservative look and is dressier than many cities. You won't often see local fellows wearing T-shirts in the evening unless you're in a sports bar, and you'll even see them dressed a bit nice while running into Home Depot. Even young boys have a closet full of polo shirts and button-downs to go with their shorts, pants and jeans.

Men often pair khakis with golf shirts or button-downs. Having on a collared shirt after 5 p.m. is all you need to fit in most anywhere. But a sports jacket or sweater vest (no tie required) and some decent shoes will make a nice impression in upscale downtown haunts.

Greenville women rarely step out in public unless they've paid attention to their appearance. You generally won't see them wearing T-shirts unless they've accessorized with a scarf. The average local gal probably owns at least two dozen scarves, the number one accessory in the 864. Get a few, and pair them with jewelry for dresses, blouses and tees if you want to look like a Greenvillian. Learning the intricacies of the scarf will pay off.

Dresses are another wardrobe staple, and are often paired with sandals or cowboy boots for football games or going downtown. Pedicures are big business here in warm months, and nearly every woman has at least one good pair of boots for winter. Cute rain boots are another popular style statement and get heavy use in January and February. Galas will necessitate a bit of formal wear, but luckily, it's easy to find (and Greenville even has a formal wear concierge).

The Language

The true Greenville accent is one of the country's most beautiful, its warmth conveyed in each drawn-out syllable. "Y'all" is definitely spoken here, and the local vernacular implies friendship, inclusion and southern hospitality. Some of the variations you'll hear—including misuse of verbs—are borne of nearby mountain and rural regions. This can drive linguistics-oriented folks a little nuts. But the truth is, some very smart people simply fall into the habit of talking this way from being around others who use the rural vernacular. Resist the urge to judge.

Southern naming conventions—two names for girls, family surnames for boys' first names—are prevalent in Greenville. And children nearly always add "Miss" or "Mister" to the first name of adults they know. Watch for contextual signals when someone says "Bless her heart." This phrase can be a way to express concern, but can also be a southerner's way of softening mention of a fault. Deciphering intent is half the fun.

16

You'll definitely hear some new words and phrases when you get here, many of which will delight your ears, and a few which will puzzle you. Here's a chart to help you make sense of it all.

You'll Hear (or See)	What It Means, or other notes
ACC	the college conference Clemson belongs to
Ben Martin	PGA golfer who lives here
bird dog	a hot dog bun with chicken strips in it
bold peanuts (boiled peanuts)	a popular roadside or convenience store snack
Carolina	can mean USC, UNC, or the two states (SC, NC)
CASH-ers (Cashiers)	a nearby resort town in western North Carolina
CHAWL-stun (Charleston)	the speaker is a native of the low country
CLIMP-sun (Clemson)	Pronounce using a missing "p" … and never a "z"
Dabo (Dă-boe)	Clemson's football coach, Dabo Swinney
Dark Corner	NW corner of county; homemade liquor heritage
Death Valley	Clemson University's football field
down at Augusta	at The Masters golf tournament
Eye-Car (CU-ICAR)	Clemson's campus for automotive research
Grrr	Greer, an adjacent community, to the NE
GREEN-vul	this pronunciation means the speaker is native
Haas	PGA family from Greenville (father Jay, son Bill)
half and half	Half French fries, half onion rings
Jo-CASS-ee	large nearby lake with protected shoreline
low country	the coast near Charleston; or its cuisine
ma'am	a sign of respect and courtesy; rarely about age
MAC-bee (McBee)	McBee St (downtown) named for Vardry McBee
meat and three	a restaurant's offering of a protein and three sides
Nikki	Nikki Haley, the state's 116th governor
old GREEN-vul (Old Greenville)	about a 1.5 mile radius from Main and Washington
SEC	the college athletic conference USC belongs to
shag	a swing-type dance done to Carolina beach music
SIR-see (sercy)	a small unexpected gift
Sparkleburg	Spartanburg
T.R.	Traveler's Rest, just north of Greenville
the ABC or Red Dot store	liquor store (regulated by Alcholic Beverage Comm.)
the Drive	The Greenville Drive MiLB team
the ham house	Tommy's Ham House, a Republican bastion
the lake	typically Lake Keowee, Jocassee or Hartwell
the Panthers	The Charlotte Panthers NFL team
the party store	the liquor store, aka "the ABC"

the Pee Dee	the northeastern part of SC, named for a river
the Swamp Rabbit	the county's bike trail
The Swamp Rabbits	the city's ECHL team, formerly the Road Warriors
up on Paris	on Paris Mountain
USC	University of South Carolina
WNC	mountain area of western NC, including Asheville
#yeahTHATgreenville	popular hashtag used on social media

A whole slew of major roads are also referred to by their numbers.

SEE ALSO: Handy Reference Section: **Roads to Know**

Passions and Opinions

While Greenvillians are respectful of beliefs other than their own, the topics on which you can count on a strong opinion being held include college football, God, the best type of BBQ sauce, the best BBQ joint, the best beach, BMW cars (yes!), Michelin tires (support your local economy!), regional history, American politics, the US military, the importance of good manners, green space, engineering, pimento cheese, a good education, deviled eggs and a good hunting dog. These opinion won't necessarily be expressed…but they will be held.

Politics

Politics within the city limits tend to be slightly more purple than red or blue, while Greenville County and most of the state lean toward red. Even if you're not typically keen on politics, you'll be entertained by the near-constant presence of (mostly) Republican presidential candidates prior to each South Carolina primary (the first in the South). You can see them in the lobby of the Poinsett Hotel, at pricey private events, at large performance venues, and at Tommy's Ham House, the city's longtime bastion of conservative politics. But no matter which way you lean, you'll be pleasantly surprised at how the Southern civility of Greenville citizens carries over into politics.

18

Greenville is a frequent stop for politicians
Photo courtesy of D.J. Henson

Football

As in most of the South, life revolves around Saturdays in fall. But throughout the entire year, it will seem that nearly half the city's residents are diehard **Clemson University** fans. You'll notice their orange clothing and the ever-present Tigers paw-print on flags, clothing, home decor, bakery items, lawns and front doors. You'll even see orange cars and orange-and-purple businesses.

The Clemson campus lies just 45 minutes to the west; countless alums, a few professors and parents of many a student live and work in Greenville. There's a strong regional loyalty to Clemson, which won "best game day ambience" in a national contest held by USA TODAY 10Best. If you want to make a quick friend of a Clemson fan, simply reference **1981**. This year marks the season in which Clemson won the national title in NCAA football. (2015 was another great year; the Tigers made it all the way to the national championship game and were barely beaten).

19

Clemson's stadium is nicknamed Death Valley, and "the rock" at the top of the stadium entrance—brought back from Death Valley by a former coach—is touched by all players as a sign of commitment as they storm in for a home game. Tailgating outside this stadium is legendary.

Another omnipresent block of team devotees wear garnet, in support of the University of **South Carolina Gamecocks**. Nearby Columbia is home to this major university, its "USC" moniker confusing for those moving here from the west. Gamecock fans also live and breathe football, and on Saturdays they fill William Brice Stadium, where parking lot tailgating is a multi-generation tradition, replete with big screen TVs, popup tents, cornhole game sets and mega-grills.

Don't make the mistake of thinking that anyone avid enough to regularly display a loyalty could not possibly be a city mover or shaker. Football is a religion here. Planning an event in the fall? Don't hold it on a Saturday if you want a big attendance. People skip weddings for football in Greenville.

On game days, cars with team flags will be pulling out of driveways as early as eight. Places selling chicken wings or beer will be busy by nine; many restaurants also offer early morning takeout on days when kickoff is at noon. **Tailgating** supplies include hot dogs, burgers, wings, ribs, pulled pork, chili ingredients, sides and beer. Grillmeister bragging rights are all part of the fun. If you're lucky enough to be invited to participate in this tradition, just say yes.

It's important to note that despite being in separate athletic conferences, Carolina and Clemson are arch enemies in the world of football. The game in which they vie for annual bragging rights—The Palmetto Bowl—is always the last of the season (typically the Saturday after Thanksgiving) before conference championship and playoff games begin. The following week, football fans must choose whether to attend the city's annual Christmas parade or one of the biggest games of the year.

High school football inspires passion too, as Greenville HS fans illustrate
Photo courtesy of Stacey Krall

Places of Worship

Spirituality plays a large role in the lives of most Greenvillians. A family's place of worship is often its social center as well; church basketball leagues are big here, and there's softball, too. While Baptist churches are omnipresent—and typically hold the highest geographic points in every community—you'll discover many other options.

Sunday morning church attendance is impressive, and eating out afterward is a local family tradition. Restaurants are typically far less busy on Wednesday nights, another popular worship time. Several area churches have their own private schools.

SEE ALSO: The Greenville Lifestyle: **Spiritual Life**

All Things Food (and Drink!)

Mountain and coastal influences have shaped Greenville's cuisine, as has Southern tradition. A further fusion of inventive chefs, the abundance of regional year-round produce, and steady influx of internationals gives the city a wealth of dining options. With fertile farmland surrounding Greenville, the locavore culture of farm-to-table dining is gaining traction, and popular local farmers markets are introducing residents to their neighbor producers and growers. Artisanal food producers are also enjoying a strong level of support.

If you're used to multi-cultural cuisines, you're in luck. Greenville has Thai, Mexican, Indian, German, Italian, Cajun, Colombian, Japanese, Vietnamese, Chinese, New Mexican, Peruvian, Soul Food and more. A wide variety of groceries and markets also make finding ethnic ingredients easy.

Market Name	Location
Asian Market	Wade Hampton Blvd
Asian Supermarket	Greenville - eastside, Orchard Park Rd
Bob & Lisa's Produce	Powdersville - Hwy 81 / Anderson Rd
Caviar & Bananas	Greenville - downtown, beneath Aloft Hotel
Earth Fare	Greenville - eastside, on Pelham Rd
European Market	Greenville - eastside, on Woodruff Rd
Fresh Market	Greenville - S. Pleasantburg at Laurens
La Unica Supermercado	Greenville - White Horse Rd
Mauldin Open Air Market	Mauldin - on Butler, next to Mauldin HS
Mill Village Market	Greenville - Lois Ave, Village of W Greenville
New York Butcher Shop	Greenville - August Rd, south of Faris
Swamp Rabbit Cafe & Grocery	Greenville - Cedar Lane Rd, near downtown
Tomato Vine	Greenville - Old Buncombe Rd, near Furman
Trader Joe's	Greenville - eastside, on Woodruff, W of I-85
Whole Foods	Greenville - eastside, on Woodruff, E of I-85

"You've got execs and leadership people here from all over the world," says pioneering restaurateur Carl Sobocinski, "people who have been to *great* restaurants. Our community supports the things that people like that *expect* in places they're going to call home." But beyond quality and variety, Greenville is

22

also about tradition, starting with its comfort foods.

Regional Foods, Customs

Two items appear on many a menu: **deviled eggs and pimento cheese**. Have fun experimenting with locally sold varieties of pimento cheese, and the dishes in which it's used (burgers, for example). Take a homemade version of either item to a party, and you'll make fast friends.

As all across the South, the requisite beverage here is **tea**. But servers in Greenville won't expect you to say "tea" and certainly not "iced tea." The question you'll get is **"sweet or unsweet."** Sound savvy, head off the question, and order your preference by adjective only. (Sweet means REALLY sweet, by the way, with lots of sugar).

Greenville might be your first exposure to the **meat-and-three** restaurant (a common business model in the South, where the main offering is a protein plus three sides). The "vegetable" list might give you the giggles in the few places where it includes mac 'n cheese or applesauce. Cornbread comes with many a meal and is often sweet (but not always).

Don't miss the opportunity to sample **collard greens** and **fried okra** in a meat-and-three. **O.J.'s Diner** is a locals' favorite. (You might run into the mayor here). Any of the **Clock, Stax** or **Pete's** diners are also a good bet, or try **Tupelo Honey**. In Greenville, you'll also come across more than one menu offering **fried chicken, fried catfish**, or the funny **chicken and waffle** combo, allegedly inspired by 4 a.m. patrons torn between dinner and breakfast.

Fun fact: The liquid produced by cooking collards is called *potlikker*.

Some Carolina residents might try to tell you you're still not a local until you love **boiled peanuts**. You should try them once…but another local food—the **fried bologna sandwich**—is much easier to love.

23

Greenville's food truck scene is alive and well
Photo courtesy of Indie Craft Parade

BBQ

Barbecue is practically a religion in the South, and Greenville is no exception. If you want to fit in, buy your own smoker, be prepared to discuss a couple of local sources for the "real stuff," or both.

The debate in the offices of Greenville-based USA TODAY 10Best is always fierce when it comes to choosing the city's ten best BBQ joints. **Bucky's**, **Henry's**, **Charlie's** and **Little Pigs** typically hold firm top spots. For a "fine dining" BBQ experience with to-die-for Southern veggie sides, head to downtown's **Smoke on the Water**.

Each spring, there's a huge **BBQ Cook-Off & Festival** held downtown: hungry citizens descend upon the competition area to eat, compare and eat some more. Nearby Spartanburg also hosts the **Hub City Hog Fest** the same month.

Fun fact: The Carolinas are distinct in that all three styles of BBQ sauce are used here: mustard-, vinegar- and tomato-based. You'll find a prevalence of the tomato-based sauce on pulled pork, but many joints offer beef and three or more sauces (including some with heat). It's perfectly acceptable to mix any that you like, and lots of folks do.

24

Downtown Dining

Downtown Greenville is bursting with over 100 dining options. To give you an idea of the variety you'll find, there's foodie Mecca **American Grocery Restaurant**; popular **Pomegranate**, with its Persian menu; **The Trappe Door**, serving Belgian style food and beer; **Larkin's on the River**, for savory steaks; **Nantucket Seafood**, where the menu holds a chilled seafood tower; and **Roost**, one of the city's 'Southern with a twist' venues. Food-centric Charleston has taken note, and perhaps its most acclaimed restaurant—**Husk**—is establishing a presence in Greenville, following in the footsteps of **Caviar & Bananas**.

Al fresco dining is part of downtown's culture
Photo courtesy of Table 301 / Soby's

Fun Fact: The aforementioned Carl Sobocinski, owner of some of the city's most popular restaurants (**Soby's, Soby's on the Side, The Lazy Goat, Nose Dive, Passarelle**) was the first restaurateur to invest in downtown in a big way. He charted the course with namesake Soby's, one of Main Street's most popular options.

Locally-Grown and Produced

While the state of South Carolina gets low marks overall on health, the success of the Upstate's Slow Food movement and many local **farmers markets**, including downtown Greenville's wonderful **TD Saturday Market**, illuminate

25

the growing desire to foster a sustainable environment for growers and producers. At farmers markets and in various retail settings, you'll discover all sorts of wonderful locally produced products: **Kuka Juice, Southern Pressed Juicery, LaRue Chocolates, Naked Pasta, King of Pops** and more.

Visit the **Greenville State Farmers Market** year-round, or one of the other **area farmers markets** (May-Oct) in **Travelers Rest, Fountain Inn** or **Simpsonville**. Watch for local farm tours, and farm-to-table suppers, which sell out quickly. There's even a **Slow Food Earth Market** held once a month (May-Nov) in Greenville. The producers at this small farmers market—the only one of its kind in the continental U.S.—are carefully vetted by members of Slow Food Upstate so the sustainably raised products sold here are free of harmful chemicals and GMOs.

Farmers markets are very popular in the Upstate
Photo courtesy of GreenvilleRelocation.com

In 2011, one visionary duo boldly transformed an abandoned building in an overlooked part of town into the now-beloved **Swamp Rabbit Cafe & Grocery**, proving it was possible to support local farmers *and* attract customers (including those on bicycles, as the cafe lies along the Swamp Rabbit Trail).

Mill Village Farms took root in 2012, turning its focus to growing affordable food on vacant land while giving disadvantaged neighborhood youth much-needed entrepreneurial skills. Today it has a mobile market, and a brick and mortar market in the Village of West Greenville.

26

More and more restaurants in Greenville are sourcing their food locally. "I see a lot of chefs working one-on-one with farmers," reveals Sobocinski. "They'll have a dish on their menu, and they'll tell the farmer they're going to need so many pounds of turnip greens over the next six months, a true win for farmers, restaurateurs, chefs and patrons. The **Greenville State Farmers Market**, open daily on Rutherford Road, actually maintains a Fresh on the Menu app which promotes restaurants sourcing locally-grown food.

Most local honey is wildflower or sourwood, but there are wide variations in color and taste. Groceries are good about carrying honey sourced from the area, but you'll also discover farmers and roadside vendors who offer it. If you want your own hives, it's easy to find help in getting started, from folks like those at **The Carolina Honey Bee Company**, in Travelers Rest.

Dough (Pastries, Crepes and Pizza)

If you get your kicks from pastries, **Legrand Bakery**, **Upcountry Provisions**, **Art Eats**, **Buttercream Bakehouse**, and **Great Harvest Bread Company** are all worthy of your patronage. Track down **Prep Confections** to taste macarons unlike any others.

Travelers Rest is home to cheery **Tandem**, a homegrown creperie offering savory and sweet plates for breakfast and lunch. Its clever owners publicly funded their launch by appealing to T.R. residents, who continue to support Tandem with a passion. As of this writing, another creperie was on the horizon in downtown Greenville.

Pizza fans devour the gourmet pies at popular **Sidewall Pizza**, with locations near downtown and in Travelers Rest. They also flock to college favorite **Mellow Mushroom** downtown.

Food Events

The annual Euphoria event has made a tremendous impact on Greenville's food scene. "When you can bring three different Michelin starred chefs here in one year, it elevates everyone around them," says co-founder Carl Sobocinski, who co-founded Euphoria with singer/songwriter Edwin McCain.

27

Restaurant Week Greenville JANUARY	Greenville Small Plate Crawl MARCH	Foodie Fest AUGUST
Restaurants offer savory and sweet three- and four-course prix-fixe meals at value prices	Restaurants serve $4-$10 portions of tantalizing tastes	Prix-fixe courses by local chefs at the city's upscale restaurants & groups
Euphoria SEPTEMBER	Fall for Greenville Festival OCTOBER	Local Supper Clubs MONTHLY
Celebrity chefs, vintners, musicians and fab foodie events. Launch events happen throughout the year so follow the festival on social media.	40+ local restaurants and breweries set up booths along Main Street. Local bands provide the entertainment.	To be in the know, watch Facebook and local food-friendly media.

Advice from a Food Writer

Greenville is blessed with passionate and talented food writers. M. Linda Lee is a former editor of The Michelin Guide and a contributing editor for TOWN Magazine, as well as a contributor to Edible Upcountry, The Local Palate and other publications which feature food. She says to be adventurous. "While downtown Greenville is chock-a-block with great places to eat," says Lee, "make sure you venture off the beaten path to places like **Stella's Southern Bistro** in Simpsonville, **Bacon Brothers Public House** on the eastside, and **Grits and Groceries** in Belton."

Lee also recommends a few foodie treks: a day trip to **Happy Cow Creamery** in Pelzer, to learn about Tom Grantham's 'four Aprils' method of grazing, or visiting **Split Creek Goat Farm** in Anderson, to sample goat cheese made on-site. She also advises heading north toward Asheville, to tour the many creameries along the Western North Carolina Cheese Trail.

Water and Coffee

Fresh from three protected mountain reservoirs, our tap water has won national awards, giving us even more bragging rights. No bottled water necessary here. Great water makes coffee even better and artisanal baristas are flocking to the area: Check out downtown's **Methodical Coffee** or community hub **Due South**, which started at Taylors Mill, but is expanding to other locations. **Coffee**

28

Underground is a favorite downtown hangout; **Spill the Beans** anchors the entrance to Falls Park, and **The Village Grind** is another aromatic stop.

Tandem creperie in T.R. is another coffee hot spot
Photo courtesy of GreenvilleRelocation.com

Spirits

Across the state of South Carolina, liquor stores—marked with a big red dot—close nightly at 7pm *sharp,* and never open on Sundays. Beer and wine are much more readily available. Within Greenville city limits, you can order a cocktail on a Sunday in any restaurant with a Sunday license. Each city has its own laws relevant to Sunday sales, but generally speaking, you'll find beer and wine available in local markets on Sunday. Restaurant options vary city to city.

Hot Tip: This issue was coming up for a vote as of this writing, so check to see if the law has changed.

At some point, you'll hear reference to **"the dark corner"** referencing the far

29

northwest corner of the state. This heavily forested, hard-to-reach area (and thus, the name) has a heritage tied to the production of homemade spirits. Stop into the award-winning **Dark Corner Distillery** to learn more about this intriguing history and the distilling process itself. You can also sample and purchase locally-made moonshine while you're there. **Six & Twenty Distillery,** in the Powdersville area, also offers tours and tastings.

Burgeoning Beer Scene

Greenville's brew culture is stronger than ever with an expanding roster of craft beer makers and the city often on the short list for larger breweries looking to expand. **The Community Tap** is a popular neighborhood hub centered around a carefully curated selection of beverages. It offers over 800 craft beers, with 20 rotating brews on tap and for sale by the flight, pint or growler. Weekly tastings and food pairings are all part of the fun, and a casual, welcoming vibe disguises how much you can actually learn here. Beers come from all over the world, brought in by six different distributors, but The Community Tap specializes in U.S. craft beer.

Co-owner Mike Okupinski explains that **Barley's Taproom** and **The Trappe Door** (the Belgian restaurant associated with and sited below Barley's) have become the epicenter of craft beer in Greenville. "They've allowed people like us to do what we want to do," says Okupinski, "stemming from the education they've provided."

Local breweries are coming online nearly faster than one can track. Veteran **Thomas Creek** just celebrated 17 years, including a silver medal win at the 2010 Great American Beer Festival. **Quest Brewing Company,** a gold medal winner at 2016's World Beer Cup, offers four year-round beers, four seasonals and a slew of specialties. Saturday afternoon tours are an option here, while they're available upon request at **Brewery 85,** which says it "marries Southern culture with traditional German brewing techniques." **Swamp Rabbit Brewery & Taproom** is a popular destination in Travelers Rest.

30

Quest Brewery, near the downtown airport, offers tours and tastings
Photo courtesy of D.J. Henson

As of this writing, **Birds Flew South** has started production and is in the process of opening a highly anticipated facility in a former mill. Okupinski also advises to be on the lookout for **Loose Reed** and **Fire Forge Crafted Beer**, while certified cicerone Gary Glancy offers what he calls "premier brewery tours and guided tastings," through his own company **The Brewery Experience**.

Upstate Craft Beer Company, on Augusta Road near downtown, brews a couple of its own beers, has other beers on tap, and serves as a homebrew shop. You can also **brew your own beer there** and they'll help you through the process. "There's actually a large home brew scene in the Upstate, including two major homebrew clubs: **Upstate Brewtopians** and **The Brew Stooges**," says Okupinski.

Barley's hosts **The Biggest Little Beer Festival** in January, using all three floors of its building, which has 35 taps upstairs. **The Community Tap Craft Beer Festival** is always a sellout each April. About 60 breweries are represented, each bringing two rare brews, and only 550 tickets are made available. May's **Brew in the Zoo** event offers patrons beer tastings, food and live music, after hours at The Greenville Zoo. **Euphoria** also has a beer tent each September.

Wine & Wineries

Victoria Valley is the only local wine producer; check out its beautiful setting (near Pumpkintown) where you can enjoy tastings, lunch and a wine-centric gift shop. Downtown's **Northampton Wines** (on Broad Street) carries a dazzling selection of wines from around the world, including at all price points. Tastings happen several times a month. In the wine bar, featured wines are sold by the glass but any bottle in the shop can be enjoyed at the bar, and the same goes for the shop's fantastic cheeses. Saturday lunches there are legendary.

The Community Tap, where co-owner Ed Buffington is a Certified Sommelier, carries a lovely selection of about 150 boutique wines, and also does tastings. "Our approach is more focused on people who are farmers first," says Buffington, who seeks out small, hand-crafted producers. A dozen wines are sold by the glass.

Other local **wine bars** include **Stellar** and rooftop bar **Sip**, both of which are downtown. You'll find a large **retail** selection of wine at **Total Wine**, **Green's**, **Whole Foods** and **Fresh Market**, while **Trader Joe's** and all area **grocery stores** maintain a stock that varies in size.

Stay Connected

To learn more about the food scene in Greenville, read, find or follow **Edible Upcountry**, **TOWN** magazine, **TheScoutGuide Greenville**, **Gap Creek Gourmet** blog, **Local Palate**, **SlowFoodUpstate** and **VisitGreenvilleSC**.

Goods & Services

Life requires too many goods and services to cover them all here, but to put your mind at ease, there's very little you'll ever need that you won't find in Greenville. Local consumers support a wonderful collection of specialty stores—everything from dog accessories and cycling gear to olive oils and eyewear. Health-conscious shoppers won't have any problem finding what they need, either; nor will readers, runners, cooks, crafters, artists or moms.

America's large **buying clubs** are here—Sam's, Costco—as well as many of the popular big-box stores. Much of the area's shopping is concentrated on **Woodruff Road**, which can have fierce traffic during Saturdays and winter holidays. Many small businesses are closed on Sundays.

Augusta Road has nice specialty shops, including Gage's
Photo courtesy of GreenvilleRelocation.com

South Carolina is fairly tax-friendly, but **sales taxes** can be high. In addition to the statewide sales tax rate of 6%, counties can levy up to 2% in additional tax. (Prescription drugs are exempt). To check the tax rate for the county you're moving to, go to tax-rates.org, click on the state, and then select "sales tax by county."

Main Shopping Areas

Downtown's **Main Street** offers shoppers an ever-expanding selection of retail therapy. **Augusta Road**, which stretches south from downtown's historic West End through Greenville's exclusive "605" zip code, offers chic boutiques, antiques, decor, gifts and gourmet food shops. As of this writing, many multi-use developments are under construction in and around the heart of the city; this will mean even more retail, particularly on or near **Stone Avenue**, which already holds several unique and popular small shops.

Hot Tip: Make a point of visiting We Took to the Woods (Stone Ave); Urban Digs (S. Wade Hampton); and The Cook's Station (Main Street).

The majority of Greenville's big box stores are strung along **Woodruff Road**, which has the traffic to prove it. New development continues there, however, and you'll find an ever-growing cadre of names you know and love: A.C. Moore, Academy Sports, Bed Bath & Beyond, Best Buy, Cabela's, Costco, Dick's Sporting Goods, Home Depot, Lowe's, Marshalls, Pier One, Sam's, Target, Total Wine, Trader Joe's, Whole Foods, World Market and many others. (Restaurant options are also endless along Woodruff).

Laurens Road is another shopping corridor, particularly near the intersection of Verdae. Laurens currently holds many discount, consignment and used goods stores, but you'll also find retailers including Stein Mart and Office Depot. Nearby **Haywood Road** holds the city's only **indoor mall** (the recently renovated Haywood Mall, adjacent to I-385), home to a few anchor department stores, Apple and dozens of other retailers. Streets immediately surrounding the mall hold stores with everything from suits and jewelry to furnishings and antiques.

Busy **Wade Hampton Road** is the corridor connecting downtown Greenville to Taylors and Greer. Along it, you'll find all sorts of fun and quirky shops, plus restaurants and big-box stores, including Lowe's, Home Depot, Staples and Wal-Mart. Be sure to explore the small shops at its very southern end (close to downtown), where you'll find some gems. **Pelham Road** has a number of intriguing retail and service opportunities near I-85, and nearby restaurant clusters offer everything from chicken salad to tacos to steaks.

Downtown Easley is working hard to attract shoppers and diners away from its newer side. Explore here and in **downtown Simpsonville**, which is also in the midst of a revitalization. **Fairview Road in Simpsonville** is where you'll find many recognizable large retailers while up-and-coming **downtown Fountain Inn** is home to several appealing small businesses, including a fantastic independent bookstore and a growler station.

Travelers Rest holds all sorts of fun and surprising shops. Pop in to The Cafe at Williams Hardware for a lovely selection of regional goods (and breakfast or lunch). Sunrift Adventures has boundless outdoor apparel and gear.

Last but not least, the **Pickens Flea Market** is legendary, not just for its immense size, but for its longevity. Go early on any Wednesday, and wear your walking shoes.

Artisans & Makers

Local style and design writer Ruta Fox points out one exciting slice of the city's population. Greenville's history as a textile hub, she explains, has made the city a natural jumping-off point for a recent influx of young makers, artisans and entrepreneurs. "Their innovative, homegrown businesses and handmade creations are infusing fresh energy into Greenville," says Fox, who moved here from Manhattan.

According to Fox, you'll find hand-sewn, made-to-order denim at **Billiam Jeans**; custom-designed women's clothing at **Yelena Exclusive Atelier**; metal necklaces from **Maritime Supply Co.**; witty T-shirts from **Dapper Ink**; and fine jewelry from gem-happy designer **Charme Silkiner**; plus a host of other independent creators whose goods are sold around town.

Fashion Brands

Ruta Fox weighs in again on where to find favorite brands: "Greenville's charming Main Street shopping includes everything from traditional **Brooks Brothers** to ultra-stylish shops and quirky **Anthropologie**," she says. Boutique-dotted **Augusta Road** and **The Shops at Greenridge** on Woodruff Road "offer a wide mix of retail," says Fox, while "anchor department stores **Dillard's**, **Belk** and **Macy's** at **Haywood Mall** carry mid-priced lines from designers such as **Ralph Lauren**, **Calvin Klein** and **Michael Kors**. You'll also find mall staples like **J. Crew** and **Banana Republic** as well as fast fashion retailer **Forever 21**."

Fox advises shoppers looking for something extravagant to make the drive to nearby SouthPark Mall in Charlotte, for deluxe shopping at **Hermes**, **Tiffany**, **Armani**, **Neiman Marcus** and **Nordstrom**.

*Hot Tip: Drop by **Wilson's on Washington** salon for an irresistible selection of affordable costume jewelry and accessories.*

Fashions & Style

Fellows who enjoy shopping for themselves should check out Greenville's high end menswear stores: **Rush Wilson, Brockman's Menswear; Smith & James; Jack Runnion;** and **Empire LTD** in downtown Greer.

National model (and Greenville resident) Fredrick Dean's style consultancy **JusDean** can painlessly help edit or update your wardrobe for life in Greenville (and elsewhere, if you travel). The JusDean team includes the ever-dashing but unintimidating Dean as well as David Gregory, Greenville's only **formal wear concierge,** who brings 40 years of experience as owner of Gregory's Formal Wear on the Go.

Style consultants David Gregory and Fredrick Dean
Photo courtesy of B. Smith Photography

Dean and Gregory specialize in tailored suits, but also direct clients toward fabrics and colors which suit the season and the person. They both consult for gentlemen, while Dean also advises women, and spends countless hours

36

editing wardrobes for both. The firm's clientele includes politicians, athletes, and professionals of all kinds. Team member Lindsie Sink specializes in **professional attire.** She also helps ladies looking for wardrobe counsel.

The city is brimming with unique **women's wear** boutiques and at a wide price range. The most surprising is downtown Greenville's clever **Pedal Chic,** which carries adorable cycling and recreation attire for gals. Boutiques worth investigating include—*but are certainly not limited to*—upscale **Cone & Coleman; Taz; Twill; Monkee's of the West End;** and **Custard.** You'll find dozens of options in three main areas: downtown, Augusta Road, and downtown Greer.

"Consignment shop **Labels** is the "go to" spot for women looking for stylish designer names at a fraction of the original price," advises Ruta Fox. "**Chanel, Helmut Lang, Giuseppe Zanotti, Prada** and **Louis Vuitton** are just a few of the top tier luxury brands that are stocked here. It's a treasure trove of clothes, shoes and accessories." Fox also likes resale boutiques **L's on Augusta, Divine Consignment, Consign Werks** and **Saige Consignment Boutique,** saying "they all offer gently worn, well-priced clothing and accessories from labels like Tahari and DKNY."

"There's no shortage of great options when it comes to kids' fashion in Greenville," says shopping expert and new mom Taryn Scher. Some of Scher's favorites include **Vann & Liv, Sassy Kids, The Petite Parade,** and **The Grey Goose.**

"When it's time to register for your major baby needs and nursery furniture, **Buy Buy Baby** and **Babies R' Us** really do have everything," advises Scher, citing Buy Buy Baby's newer brands and really unique product lines. "**Baby Furniture Plus Kids** has beautiful custom options," she says, "but they can come with a hefty price tag." Scher directs parents and grandparents to locally owned **toy stores O.P. Taylor's** and **The Elephant's Trunk,** which offer "a great selection."

Personal Care & Aesthetics

The city has no shortage of inviting day spas, many of which provide massage, facials and mani-pedis. **Massage Envy** also enjoys a healthy presence across the Upstate. **Solace Skincare,** on Pelham west of Haywood, is a best bet for waxing. Multiple clinics about the city offer personal aesthetic services, from rejuvenation injections to cool sculpting. Men can enjoy a straight razor shave at **Bo Stegall** on Stone Avenue, or at **Frank's** downtown, where they'll also pour you a drink.

Furnishings, Antiques, Art and Designers

The Greenville area is home to several recognizable furniture stores—**Ethan Allen, Bassett, Broyhill, Haverty's, La-Z-Boy, Rooms to Go** and **Pier One** among them—but you'll also discover several unique places from which to furnish your new home. The influx of new residents to Greenville, and the sheer volume of home construction and renovation going on here, has been the catalyst for all sorts of exciting new options in the design world.

Four factors make furnishing your new home exciting:

1. The area has a wealth of **interior designers** who can help you navigate the process of creating a new home. (Designers also have access to major **furniture markets** in nearby Atlanta, High Point, Hickory and Charlotte).
2. Our proximity to North Carolina's **furniture-making region** delivers opportunity for savings.
3. Its textile heritage has given Greenville a permanent love of **beautiful fabrics**; great fabric shops abound.
4. A steady stream of **talented artisans** are moving here and making beautiful one-of-a-kind furnishings.

"Greenville really has an extraordinary array of resources, from artists to antique stores," says interior designer David Watkins. "For those people wanting something truly special, the resources are much more than what people see on the surface."

Hot Tip: David Watkins Designs' full list of go-to contractors can be found online at GreenvilleRelocation.com.

Unique Furnishing and Design Sources

Here's a handy chart to help you find furnishings and/or design help for your new home:

38

New	Antiques or Repurposed	Consign	Business Name	Designer(s)
✓			4 Rooms	✓
	✓		Antiques on Augusta	✓
✓			Bogari	
✓			Carolina Furniture & Interiors	✓
	✓	✓	Consign & Design	
			Dalton Interiors	✓
			David Watkins Designs	✓
			Elizabeth Mann Designs	✓
✓	✓		Eric Brown Design	✓
	✓	✓	Feather Your Nest	
✓			Foothills Furniture	
✓			Fowler Interiors	✓
	✓		Galleries of Brian Brigham	✓
			Gary Hester Interiors	✓
	✓		Greystone Antiques	
	✓		Knack	
✓	✓		Mayme Baker Studio	✓
✓			Old Colony Furniture Co.	✓
✓	✓		Postcard from Paris	✓
✓	✓		Rowan Company Furniture	✓
	✓	✓	Southern Housepitality	
	✓		The Rock House Antiques	✓
	✓		Trade Route Imports	
✓	✓		Vintage Now Modern	✓

If you love **fine art**, don't fail to seek out **Hampton III Gallery**, which specializes in collectible regional artists of many mediums and styles; **Bennetts Frame and Art Gallery**, with its wonderful selection of contemporary pieces, including Greenville scenes; and downtown's evocative **Mary Praytor Gallery**, where affordable jewelry and avant-garde art cozy up to more traditional investment pieces.

Should additional design resources merit a road trip, seek out **Architectural Warehouse in Tryon, NC** (its smaller version is in Landrum, SC); **Charlotte's design district** (South Blvd.); the furniture and design shops of **downtown**

Hendersonville (NC) and Asheville; Togar Rugs in Asheville; and Rug and Home in Gaffney. Atlanta's design district is a little farther but worth a trip.

Our Internationals

Greenville is hardly your typical Southern city. Nearly 30 countries have international firms located in the county, among them the massive BMW Manufacturing plant, and Michelin's United States headquarters. So you'll hear *"bonjour"* and *"auf wiedersehen"* without even trying. Students at Clemson's International Center for Automotive Research and USC's medical school add to the cultural diversity of the area.

One amazing resource—the dynamic **Upstate International**—is at the heart of it all, its two-fold mission to connect international people with a community, and to engage South Carolinians with the international community. Both goals are accomplished by connecting people through events, programs and other initiatives that foster the dynamic exchange of international culture and ideas. For people who've moved here from other countries—many of them as a 'trailing spouse'—the organization's role is truly critical: while one person goes to work, the family is often left to 'figure things out'. "A spouse and children have a lot more integration that needs to happen," explains Executive Director Tracie Frese. "They can be part of the community and happy to stay…or they can be left behind. Our goal is to make sure when someone calls here with a question, we can find an avenue for them."

Fun Fact: Our state was recently ranked fourth in the USA, in the percent of private-industry employment in foreign companies.

This idea of a support system for internationals got an early boost from Michelin, then the City and Clemson got involved. **Relocation services** were developed and **Language classes** started being offered—including ESL (English as a second language). Today, you can study **German, French, Italian, Spanish, Russian** and **Chinese** at the Center.

40

Goods at European Market on Woodruff Road
Photo courtesy of D.J. Henson

The organization's slogan—'South Carolina including the world'—is never truer than at the inspiring, free and fun-filled **Salsa at Sunset** events hosted by UI in downtown Greenville. People of all sizes, shapes and colors joyfully dance the night away, together.

Membership is inexpensive and a fun way to meet people, especially if you love travel, language, culture, learning or people. UI members enjoy a myriad of opportunities. "Our members do **hikes**, **biking**, **coffees**, **lunches**, and have an **international book club**," says Frese. "Members can also attend a once-monthly meeting here, with a program. We do a beaujolais dinner every fall, and a gluehwein party once a year." The organization has both an **international women's club** and an **international men's club**.

Surprisingly, there are several schools in Greenville in which children can learn in their native tongue, helping them retain this critical language skill. Blythe Academy of Languages, the Greenville County 'Select' magnet school which offers daily foreign language instruction to all its K5-5 students, has both French and Spanish immersion.

Country Contacts & Cultural Groups

Upstate International maintains an **online list of contacts** who can answer

41

questions, arrange for help and facilitate engagement with the local community from over **two dozen countries**: Belgium, Finland, Turkey, Peru, India, Haiti, Norway and others. Dozens of international organizations are also listed on its resource list, including Alliance Francaise, Chinese Culture and Education Center, Italian American Club, Ballet Folklorico and Swiss-American Society of the Piedmont.

"We really want to build connections, to be a bridge between groups," says Frese, "and that's what's different about us. We're not culture specific. We try to be a hub."

Fun Fact: Greenville Hospital Systems utilizes a team of in-house translators to translate a wide variety of documents, so that patients with limited or no English language skills have access to materials they need for their care.

International Events

Local festivals and celebrations include the Greenville Scottish Games, the Greek Festival, Oktoberfest, Hispanic Festival, and A Day with India, as well as the Shinnenkai, the Bon Japanese festival and the World Tai Chi Day.

Weather & Seasons

The choice to put down roots in the Carolinas is a great one. Greenville's enviable location in the Blue Ridge foothills gives it some protection from wintry weather while affording it with comfortable summers. Asheville, just an hour north, has tremendously different temperatures than Greenville does: up there, cold months pack freezing temps and blustery winds. Columbia, an hour and a half south of our city, suffers through much more heat and humidity, its summers often described as "brutal."

Summer can certainly contain some hot days, but you'll be so busy having fun outdoors, you'll barely notice. Golf, tennis, boating, cycling, hiking, paddling… Greenville's beautiful environs are incredibly inviting in the year's warm months. Evenings are often pleasant enough to dine outdoors and area restaurants with outdoor seating stay in demand.

42

Many Greenville folks take off for a week during summer and head to their **favorite beach**. The coast is only three hours away, so you'll hear new friends talking about Litchfield, Pawley's Island, Isle of Palms, Edisto, Hilton Head and other coastal destinations. You'll enjoy discovering which beach is "your" beach.

Hot Tip: The transitional autumn weeks just after school starts are also a great time to hit the shore if you're able.

Photo courtesy of D.J. Henson

Once your friends start discovering the magic of **autumn** in Greenville, you'll need a guest room. Our deciduous trees start doing their thing each October and by late in the month, kaleidoscopic color blankets the city. Factor in the lush greens of winter rye—a popular lawn choice—and even non-photographers are inspired.

Best of all, places like Caesars Head, Sassafras Mountain, apple orchards and the famed Blue Ridge Parkway are all within a short drive. Fall, with its crisp nights, sunny days, and gorgeous color is nothing short of magical in Greenville and nearby areas.

Winters will include a snowfall now and then, but certainly not the lasting kind. (There can be rare ice, so keep that in mind when looking at homes with steep driveways). Leaves typically drop around the first of November, but temps can still occasionally soar into the low 70s on the occasional December day. The only truly tedious winter months are January and February, which can bring cold rain.

Before you know it, March will arrive it all its flora glory. **Spring** is legendary in the Deep South and Greenville is no exception. A drive through nearly any neighborhood will reveal bountiful azaleas and daffodils, while country roads will be lined with orange tiger lilies. Accompanying all those blossoms is a bounty of pollen. Expect any unsheltered car to turn lime green for a few weeks from mid-March to mid-April. If you're susceptible, buy over-the-counter allergy meds a month early; they can run out of stock.

Spring is magnificent in Greenville
Photo courtesy of GreenvilleRelocation.com

Here's a look at the average **TEMPERATURES** in the area:

JAN	FEB	MAR	APR	MAY	JUN	JUL	AUG	SEPT	OCT	NOV	DEC
40	43	52	60	68	75	78	77	71	61	52	43

Pleasant **RAINFALL** keeps the green in Greenville. This chart shows average inches of rain per month in the area:

JAN	FEB	MAR	APR	MAY	JUN	JUL	AUG	SEPT	OCT	NOV	DEC
3.82	3.97	4.52	3.36	3.76	3.8	4.8	4.48	3.43	3.44	3.7	4.11

HUMIDITY makes cool temperature feel cooler, so if you move here from out west, you might feel it, but monthly averages vary little from 54% throughout the year.

44

CHAPTER 2:
GREENVILLE'S WOW FACTORS

Award-Winning Downtown

Downtown is very likely the thing that drew you to Greenville, and your opinion is shared. Travel & Leisure magazine placed Greenville in its Top Ten list of 'America's Greatest Main Streets.' It's where many a dream begins, the dream of moving to this great city. It's easy to imagine taking your own friends to **Falls Park** on their first visit to see you, and watching their reaction. For some, it's downtown's **great restaurants**, or the abundance of **free outdoor concerts** held there, while others love our **TD Saturday Market**.

Downtown Greenville was reimagined to be inspiring
Photo courtesy of D.J. Henson

The love affair with Greenville is boosted by great shows at the **Peace Center** and the **Greenville County Museum of Art**, and by the chance to take a romantic stroll along the Reedy River, stopping when a swing for two is open and beckoning. Greenville's downtown has almost won more awards than you can count.

It might not surprise you, then, that Greenville is visited by civic leaders from across the USA, who come for ideas they can implement back home. Residents and visitors flock to downtown, driving in from all over the Upstate, to enjoy the **restaurants, performance venues, galleries and unique shops** flourishing on or near a twinkling tree-lined Main Street.

Festivals of all kinds add another layer of recreation to many a weekend, while **The Swamp Rabbit Trail** acts as a year-round magnet for outdoor enthusiasts, families, cyclists, seniors, dog-walkers…you name it. Want to explore without hauling your bike? Several bike shops offer rentals.

If you prefer to relax while taking it all in, the City of Greenville's **free trolley service** runs between **Fluor Field**, with its popular **Greenville Drive baseball games**, and the North Main area, which offers even more shopping and dining options. Trolleys make a continuous loop from Greenville's historic West End to North Main, and riders can hop on and hop off. (Signs mark the 20 or so stops along the route).

Downtown also holds several city-owned, **inexpensive parking garages**, which always offer the first hour of parking free.

Hot Tip: The Richardson Street garage is free all weekend, and the West Washington Street parking deck is free on nights and weekends.

Horse and carriage rides are a wonderful way to traverse downtown, or opt for a ride from an energetic and entertaining **pedicab** driver. The city-sponsored **bike share program B-cycle** offers yet another avenue for exploration, with bike stations across downtown.

A **public art** commission oversees Main Street's many visual surprises, from Mice on Main to quotations etched in sidewalks.

"Future residents make their decision to move here while they're on Main Street," says Mayor White. "They realize they're in a place unlike any other city." It's no accident, this downtown that everyone loves. "What we tried to do," Mayor White explains, "is create a people-centered, walkable downtown. Everything flows from that."

47

Upstate International's 'Salsa Under the Stars' event
Photo courtesy of D.J. Henson

"The two transforming acts," he says, of what is now a nationally renowned revitalization, "were **trees and water**. You can't get more elementary than that." The current mayor is referring in part to the lovely shade trees lining Main Street, a project spearheaded by former Mayor Max Heller.

It was Mayor White who championed the removal of a concrete overpass which had covered the falls for 40 years, dedicating himself to the collaborations and negotiations necessary for making **Falls Park** and the **Liberty Bridge** happen. It took the commitment of many visionary people across the city to showcase these two perfectly paired features—one natural, one by design—and today they are the centerpiece of downtown and a point of real pride.

Photo courtesy of D.J. Henson

Hot Tip: Pick up a copy of 'Reimagining Greenville: Building the Best Downtown in America,' by John Boyanoski and Mayor Knox White.

48

There are many fascinating results of city leadership's focus on residential development after the falls were complete, including condos tied into the baseball field, and apartments with a private passageway to a downtown shopping center.

Fun Fact: Even downtown's manhole covers are beautiful, graphically illustrating that the city's lifeblood is its river.

A downtown sign shows the city's "watery" logo, and dining options
Photo courtesy of GreenvilleRelocation.com

2015 ushered in another phase of evolution, in which cranes filled the skyline. Construction projects literally dominated downtown. **Luxury condos, apartments, hotels and mixed use developments** all broke ground, started to rise, or actually opening, heralding Greenville's solid footing as both a **tourist destination and desirable city to live in** (none of which hurt its allure as an **innovative business hub**).

Clemson University's graduate program and the recently announced presence of USC Upstate in downtown are part of the energy. The ONE Building and adjacent ONE City Plaza have attracted all sorts of new businesses and entities, from the **Aloft Hotel** to **Anthropologie**. Restaurants and businesses from Charleston are securing space downtown. They join the 120 one-of-a-kind restaurants within a 10-block area. **Tech startups and incubators** are there too. National articles about downtown appear on a regular basis. About **4,000 people are projected to be living in the heart of the city** and supporting the ever-growing cache of interesting businesses which open there. "Now retail has followed that development," says the mayor, "and it contributes to the walking experience and makes downtown an interesting and vibrant place to be."

49

A perennial favorite—**Mast General Store**—added to Main Street's charm early on, with its old fashioned candy store, homespun goods, and aspirational outfitter gear relevant to the nearby mountains. The wondrous **O.P. Taylor's** toy store is another popular stop.

During winter **holidays**, green space at downtown's Courtyard by Marriott is transformed into an ice rink, and **Ice on Main** brings out families and friends for several weeks, all skating beneath the city Christmas tree. (Rental skates and hot chocolate are available). The Christmas **parade** happens right on Main Street, and after every Friday night home game during baseball season, Greenville Drive fans are treated to a **fireworks** show. Does it get any better?

*Hot Tip: In the ground level of City Hall (the tall, brown building) is the **VisitGreenvilleSC visitor center**, where you'll find brochures, maps, literature and friendly answers to many questions.*

Look West

Downtown is growing to the west, and the city's Salvation Army **Ray & Joan Kroc Corps Community Center** (aka The Kroc Center) is the anchor to a bright future. This community center, which sits on the Reedy River and Swamp Rabbit Trail, provides educational and recreational opportunities to the transitional neighborhood now brimming with activity and potential. The Kroc has an Olympic pool, gym, computer room, chapel, nationally recognized tennis center and a soccer field.

Plans are being made to expand park space along the Reedy. In the next few years, the Swamp Rabbit Trail from downtown will run through the middle of beautiful green space on this west side, in an emerging neighborhood of new houses and offices.

Innovative Business Environment

Greenville is a hot spot for business. "From Shanghai to London," explains Mayor Knox White, of the Greenville area, "people see us as the **Charlanta megaregion**. Being on I-85, between Charlotte and Atlanta, we're in one of the

50

highest-growth corridors in the world," he adds. "Not just in this country…but the *world*."

So there's *that*. But Greenville's success is grounded in a pro-business culture that takes full advantage of a strategic location, plus an entrepreneurial spirit and rich cultural and recreational offerings. Careful and deliberate planning—for which the city has become renowned—ensures that Greenville's growth pressures does not damage its quality of life, while its assets and direction appeal to business leaders.

"The City's leadership, along with economic development partners from the county, region and state, consistently joins with the private sector to ensure Greenville remains a place where business can grow and prosper," says Nancy Whitworth, Deputy City Manager for the City's economic development office. Whitworth (who was instrumental to this chapter's content) manages a department that drives the city's economic success and win-win partnerships. Her sincere passion for the city is also evident.

"There's an energy you can feel and see here," she says, and she's right. The Greenville community is vibrant and thriving, from its award-winning downtown to its think tanks, innovation campuses and niche manufacturing facilities. All are well-planned and -executed. Greenville serves as the economic center of South Carolina's Upstate, a jewel in the crown of this **right-to-work** state.

Officials and leaders in the Upstate region recognize that a successful economy is dependent upon 'quality of place,' keeping that in mind as each decision is made, whether it's replacing an ugly four-lane overpass with a beautiful downtown footbridge, or developing a relevant workforce that will not only thrive, but attract the right kind of business. The Greenville area grows smartly.

Greenville is Proactive

The award-winning downtown you know today is not Greenville's first major success as a city. The city's roots are in textile manufacturing, beginning on a small scale along the banks of the Reedy River and growing into global renown. By the 1920s, our city was referred to as the "Textile Center of the South" and decades later, Greenville earned the heady moniker "Textile Capital of the World."

51

This strong manufacturing heritage drew **international investment** to the Upstate from an early date. Visitors from overseas came here to buy, sell and to study manufacturing techniques. Residents often hosted those visitors in their homes, establishing personal and business ties. That welcoming spirit, combined with a pro-business environment and a solid work ethic, propelled—and continues to propel—Greenville toward the growth and success it enjoys today.

The area's transformation from textile capital to a premier destination for a **diverse industry base** has deliberately evolved. As the textile industry began collapsing, this area's automotive industry was taking off. Greenville purposefully set out to ensure a diverse base, a proactive move that changed its course.

The industries which make up today's Greenville draw a **younger, educated adult population**, and offer a fantastic variety of job opportunities, adding fuel to the fiery local economy. "We've attracted a *lot* of talented younger people, impressive for a city our size," says Mayor White.

The city and its leaders are still very much looking ahead, to what should come next. Hank Hyatt, VP of Economic Development at the Greenville Chamber of Commerce, reveals there's now a focus on attracting companies working in **lightweight materials, vehicular electronics integration and composites.** "Those are three key things to drive our future," he says.

Businesses in several surrounding counties have a major positive impact on Greenville's economy and quality of life. Depending on where you choose to live, and/or if you're willing to commute, there are tremendous additional career opportunities just minutes from Greenville. Workers commute easily among Upstate counties, so it's possible (and easy) to live in Greenville County and work nearby, or vice versa, and many people do.

Michelin North America, on Greenville's east side, and **BMW Manufacturing Corporation**, with its 4,400 employees, (just across the **Spartanburg County** line), both define the Greenville area. GSP airport also lies within Spartanburg County, and has a Greer address.

52

Here's a look at the area's largest employers:

Largest Employers in Greenville, Spartanburg & Anderson Counties		
Company / Organization	Product/Service	County
State of South Carolina	State government	multi
Greenville Hospital System	Health Services	Greenville
Greenville County Schools	Public Education	Greenville
Michelin North America Inc	HQ / R&D / Mfg (radial tires)	multi
BMW Manufacturing Corp	Automobile manufacturing	Spartanburg
Bi-Lo	Corporate Headquarters	Greenville
Spartanburg Regional Health Services	Health Services	Greenville
Milliken & Company	Textile Manufacturing	multi
Bon Secours St. Francis Health System	Health Services	Greenville
AnMed Health	Health Services	Anderson
GE Power & Water	Turbines & Jet Engine Parts	Greenville
MAU Workforce Solutions	Employment services	Greenville
Wal-Mart Stores	Retail Sales	multi
US Government	Federal Government	multi
Fluor Corporation	Engineering / Construction	Greenville
Sealed Air Corp - Cryovac Division	Plastic Bags	Spartanburg
Timken US Corporation	Ball & Roller Bearing Mfg	multi
Human Technologies Inc.	Employment services	Greenville
Greenville County Government	Government	Greenville
Charter Communications	Telcom	Greenville
Anderson School District 5	Public Education	Spartanburg
Duke Energy Corporation	Energy	multi
Bob Jones University	Higher Education	Greenville
Spartanburg County Government	Government	Spartanburg
Verizon Wireless	Telecom	Greenville
Robert Bosch LLC	Automotive components	Anderson
Spartanburg County School District 6	Public Education	Spartanburg
TD Bank	Financial Services	Greenville
Spherion Staffing LLC	Telecom	Greenville

Source: Upstate SC Alliance (compiled from GSA Business, Hoovers, Infomentum, GADC)

53

International Companies

Today the South Carolina Upstate is home to more than **375 international companies from 31 countries** around the world. While France, Germany, Japan, Sweden and the U.K. factor heaviest on the list, Belgium, China, Italy, The Netherlands and Canada are not insignificant. You'll also discover Brazil, Greece, Malaysia, Ireland, Norway and even tiny Bermuda and BVI on the list of countries which have concerns doing business here. **Upstate SC Alliance** maintains a full list on its website.

Greenville's international business community also relies on the area's numerous special schools, in which kids can learn in their native tongue, thus retaining language skills while here in the USA. They include Michelin French School, Chinese Saturday School, Korean Saturday School, Japanese Saturday School and Germany Saturday School.

SEE ALSO: Getting Oriented: **Our Internationals**

Innovation and Partnerships

Greenville's **culture of innovation** spans manufacturing, education, healthcare and medical technology, telecommunications, financial services, IT, engineering and customer service industries. The city's entrepreneurial spirit is best reflected in successful and unique collaborations between the public and private sectors.

Greenville has also enjoyed **philanthropic efforts** which have consistently propelled it forward. Generous families, foundations and businesses have funded countless life-enriching projects across the Upstate, from The Peace Center and Timmons Arena, to museums and parks.

Automotive, Aviation and Transportation Innovation

There's an eye-popping 250-acre campus that calls Greenville home; you may have seen it from I-85. **Clemson University's International Center for Automotive Research (CU-ICAR)** was created as a premier automotive research, innovation and educational enterprise. Clemson's grad students for

54

automotive engineering benefit from the many corporate partnerships which keep ICAR brimming with excitement. BMW, Koyo JTEKT, Michelin, Bosch and Sage Automotive Interiors are just a few of the research partners.

South Carolina has long, strong ties to aviation. The **South Carolina Technology and Aviation Center (SC-TAC)**, sited on the former Donaldson Air Force Base, is responsible for the airfield's transformation into another innovative campus—in its own words, 'a global breeding ground for innovative research, advanced manufacturing and economic development.' It's anchored by over 90 companies, including major global players Lockheed Martin, 3M, Michelin, and Crucible Chemical Company.

Located on the SC-TAC campus, **International Transportation Innovation Center (ITIC)** provides a venue for real-world testing of transportation innovations and technologies. ITIC offers transportation research companies asphalt and concrete straightaways, a multi-lane underpass/overpass interstate, an urban city track and other features which create true testing and simulation environments. A partnership with CU-ICAR offers further advantages.

South Carolina's Inland Port is in greater Greenville
Photo courtesy of SC Port Authority

One Upstate asset is a game-changer on the logistics and transportation front. **South Carolina's Inland Port,** located in Greer (and visible on takeoff from GSP), works with 19 of the top 20 container lines in the world. It allows cargo to clear

55

customs right here—211 miles inland—before making a quick one-day trip by rail to the coast, saving valuable time for shippers.

Biomedical Technology

Clemson University Biomedical Engineering Innovation Campus (CUBE Inc.) develops high-impact medical technology and devices for disease management and technology transfer by linking graduate bioengineering students with corporate partners. Located at the Patewood campus of Greenville Health System, Clemson's CUBE Inc. keeps South Carolina at the forefront of innovative biomedical improvements.

Located at the Memorial campus of Greenville Health System, **Institute for Translation Oncology Research (ITOR)** provides some of the most advanced cancer treatments in the world by facilitating pioneering research that develops and delivers innovative, personalized cancer therapies. It is fully integrated with Greenville Health System, the Cancer Centers of the Carolinas, the pharmaceutical industry, research universities and private companies. A number of private companies are also located on the GHS campus.

Technology

For timely updates on the city's fast-changing tech landscape, find the business-oriented publications listed on the Media page in this book's Handy Reference Section.

The Iron Yard is cranking out software and web developers from its Greenville campus. This intensive 12-week school also serves as headquarters for all 17 Iron Yard schools, scattered across the US and in London. Its network of instructors, developers, designers, board members and hiring partners connect people with life-altering skills and new careers.

Greenville's internationally recognized **NEXT program**, a wholly owned and funded subsidiary of the Greenville Chamber of Commerce, is dedicated to growing and attracting high-impact, technology companies by developing the needed ecosystem and then connecting companies to that ecosystem. "There are 175 companies we work with, in the NEXT program," says Chamber VP Hank

Hyatt. "We support high-impact, high-growth companies, particularly those in life science, advanced materials or advanced manufacturing."

NEXT, in partnership with entrepreneurs, community and business leaders and partner organizations offers a number of innovative programs such as NEXT Intern Greenville, NEXT High School, MIT Mentoring Program, CEO Forums, talent attraction and retention. NEXT, along with private partners, also supports space for its tech companies in its NEXT Technology Center, NEXT on Main and the NEXT Manufacturing Center.

Greenville Chamber of Commerce's NEXT Center
Photo courtesy of GreenvilleRelocation.com

Greenville Chamber of Commerce

The city's standout Chamber of Commerce is focused on business growth, economic competitiveness and leadership development in ways that have tangible, long-lasting impact. This dynamic organization connects people, and helps them get integrated with leadership in the community. The Chamber also works in tandem with the city, helping to attract and develop world-class talent and businesses. "We're deeply engaged in realizing the future of our community," says Hyatt. "It's easy for people to plug in, and be part of making a difference."

57

Greenville Area Development Corporation (GADC)

The GADC, founded by Greenville County Council in 2001 to further economic growth, is another tremendous asset. Its support of economic initiatives has contributed to $3 billion in capital investment. Importantly, the GADC serves as a liaison between client companies and various community entities. GADC is the only local-level organization with legislative authority to negotiate incentives for new or expanding companies. It works with site selection teams, business executives, community leaders and government agencies.

The Role of Educational Partnerships

"A successful economy demands excellence in educational attainment and workforce development," explains Deputy City Manager Whitworth. "Greenville demonstrates the effectiveness of innovative partnerships to ensure those needs are met, and points to a few more key educational partnerships as proof."

In continuing the strong partnership between Clemson University and the City of Greenville, Clemson has moved its entire MBA and related graduate level programs to downtown Greenville's ONE building. Its graduate program in the heart of the city creates a synergy between local businesses and well-educated grads motivated to continue living in Greenville.

Clemson's **Center for Corporate Learning** also has a home in the upper floors of the ONE building, as does the Arthur M. Spiro Institute for Entrepreneurial Leadership and the Greenville branch of the Clemson Regional Small Business Development Center.

Greenville Technical College (GTC), with its four campuses, offers affordable technical degrees which are relevant to local industry. Since 1962, it has been adapting, growing and changing to meet the needs of the local business community. With an academic focus on business, technology and health/wellness, GTC offers degrees in 18 different tech fields, including electronics engineering, aircraft maintenance and mechanical engineering. Its health and wellness curriculum is equally rich.

The school also offers a few arts & sciences and public service degrees. "Greenville

58

Technical College is ready to support your move to Upstate South Carolina," says Dr. Keith Miller, President. "Through our graduates, companies find the well-qualified workforce they need to relocate and to grow."

To develop and sustain the requisite skill set required to support the area's advanced manufacturing base, Greenville Technical College and Clemson University have collaborated to develop the **Center for Manufacturing Innovation (CMI)**, to be located on the Millennium campus adjacent to CU-ICAR.

Designed to inspire and create rapid-entry careers in advanced manufacturing, the CMI is expected to be the first of its kind at a two-year college. The CMI will also provide area manufacturers with services including research; lab and equipment use; short technical courses; 3D printing capability; virtual reality capability; and even incubator office space.

SEE ALSO: Greenville's Assets: **Higher Education**

The opening of the four-year **University of South Carolina School of Medicine** at Greenville Health System's main campus is tied to another smart growth plan. Having seen substantial investment dollars and jobs brought to Greenville by the clustering of innovation-focused corporations in the 500+ acre CU-ICAR and Millennium campus area, city leaders and influencers are enthusiastically discussing creation of a similar **medical innovation corridor**, which would result in even more partners, investors, jobs and renown. Hank Hyatt, of the Greenville Chamber, sums up the concept by repeating a Jim Clinton quotation: "We are a community too restless to be content with our own success."

This is *not* a passive city—it's a melting-pot community of genteel, supportive, patriotic folks, who live by the put-your-money-where-your-mouth-is philosophy, who go "all in" for the things they believe in, be they family, business, church or sports. Your company can benefit from this same level of passion and commitment, while reaping the benefits of being in the heart of popular Charlanta.

Parks and Green Space

Downtown Greenville's beautiful **Falls Park** is the catalyst for many a dream of moving here. This spectacular green space is well deserving of the accolades which have been heaped upon it. It's hard to believe a four-lane overpass used to cover the falls, which, along with the **Liberty Bridge**, are now the heart of Greenville. Now the thrill of introducing visitors to the falls will be yours.

The city's Cleveland Park offers green space and trails
Photo courtesy of GreenvilleRelocation.com

The city's beloved **Swamp Rabbit Trail**, winding through the park, affords pedestrian and bicycle access to **Cleveland Park**, the massive green space adjacent to downtown. Maintained by the City of Greenville, this 122-acre urban oasis holds **The Greenville Zoo**, several playgrounds, tennis and volleyball courts, softball fields, walking and bike trails, lots of wide open space, picnic pavilions, memorials and photographers' favorite Rock Quarry Park, with its own little waterfall. And as of this writing, the very special **Cancer Survivors Park** was being created between the Church Street bridge and Cleveland Street. **38 other parks** are presently under the city's care, offering everything from **disc golf** and mini golf to tennis and kids' playgrounds.

A terrific collection of **55 *additional* parks** are the provenance of the county's impressive **Greenville Rec** department. In addition to managing all its green space, the Greenville Rec team also oversees an **ice rink**, an **inline rink**, a **camp and retreat center**, **dirt bike trails**, six **historic sites**, eight **community centers**, and the 18.6 mile **Swamp Rabbit Trail**.

Summertime fun is had at Greenville Rec's **three water parks**, all in convenient areas of the county. **Discovery Island, 7th Inning Stretch**, and **Otter Creek** each provide a unique brand of excitement with components including FlowRider®, a funnel slide and a variety of other slide options.

Summer fun at a Greenville Rec water park
Photo courtesy of Greenville County

As you explore parks in the Greenville area, you'll discover **fishing lakes**, walking trails, a **bounce house, a dog park, senior centers**…recreation options are endless, no matter your age. There's even an **aquatic center** with an indoor 20-lane 50-meter competition pool, and an indoor five-lane 25-yard heated therapy pool. Horse people will also discover **equestrian facilities**.

Greenville Rec offers kids a total of eight different **day camps**, winter and spring break camps, **after-school** programs, Kids Night Out, and a nine-week **homeschool P.E.** program.

Special Needs

Since 1968, Greenville Rec's **Camp Spearhead** has given special needs youth

61

(8+) and adults the opportunity to go to camp. Offering both residential and weekend options, this heartwarming opportunity now hosts campers at the county's impressive **Pleasant Ridge Camp & Retreat Center** on Highway 11, in the northern part of the county.

Special needs kids can also participate in their choice of Greenville Rec's **Weekend Programs**. These fun-filled outings can be anything from a Clemson basketball game or a Wild West dance party. The department also has two full-time staffers managing the county's **Special Olympics**.

The Pavilion recreation complex in Taylors is home to a **Boundless Playground**. The **Swamp Rabbit Trail** is accessible from parking lots across the Upstate and is wide enough to accommodate wheelchairs as well as people moving in the opposite direction.

Healthcare

You won't need to worry about the quality of healthcare in your new city. You'll find **world-class doctors, clinics and care** in the Upstate.

Three major hospital systems serve the greater Greenville area. You'll also find two cancer centers, a respected children's hospital, a renowned orthopedic clinic, and even an ALS clinic. Greenville Memorial is home to a **school of medicine** for the University of South Carolina, while Greenville Technical College offers one of the largest **nursing schools** in the state.

Greenville Health System (GHS) has met the Upstate's healthcare needs for more than 100 years while also serving as an academic leader in developing the next generation of healthcare providers. GHS is the state's largest not-for-profit healthcare system and an advocate for healthy living initiatives, such as LiveWell Greenville, the GHS Swamp Rabbit Trail and Greenville B-cycle, the city's bike share program. GHS also serves as a health resource for the community and a leader in transforming the delivery of health care for the benefit of the people and communities served.

As an academic health center, GHS is committed to medical excellence through

62

clinical care, education and research. From preventive medicine and routine procedures to ongoing treatment and complex surgeries, GHS is equipped with the expertise and facilities to help patients achieve total health. Its highlights include:

- Clinical University, a unique partnership with Clemson, Furman and USC
- Greenville Memorial Hospital, a Baby-Friendly designated facility
- **The GHS Cancer Institute**, one of 34 programs in the United States participating in the National Cancer Institute's Community Oncology Research Program (NCORP).

GHS locations—hospitals, physician practices, emergency centers and specialized facilities—are conveniently positioned throughout the Upstate. Its eight locations include Greenville Memorial (near Augusta Road), Patewood (Eastside), Greer, Simpsonville, North Greenville (Travelers Rest), Laurens County, Oconee Medical Campus and Baptist Easley Hospital (of which GHS is 50% owner).

GHS also has four **MD360 locations** that provide high-quality, convenient care when you experience unexpected illnesses, injuries or need common lab tests or sports physicals. MD360 sites are **open late and on weekends**.

Bon Secours St. Francis Health System is the other major hospital system based in our area. The five campuses of this not-for-profit health system have garnered some of the highest patient satisfaction ratings in the USA. Patients can visit the downtown campus; St. Francis Eastside; St. Francis Millennium; St. Francis Outpatient Center; and the Upstate Surgery Center.

Services include physician and specialty care, diagnostics, counseling, homecare, geriatrics and hospice. Faith-based Bon Secours' mission is to "bring compassion to health care," especially to those who are poor or dying. Founded by 12 compassionate French women following the French Revolution, the original congregation crossed the Atlantic shortly thereafter and established convents in the States, providing the world' first recorded formal home health care service and early day care.

Pelham Medical Center also serves the area with its eastside location, and offers an award-winning concierge approach to medical care. While actually part of Spartanburg Regional Healthcare System, Pelham Medical offers nearly

63

everything you'll need right here in the Greenville area, including a 48-bed acute-care facility and ER, along with numerous medical practices, a breast center, and **Gibbs Cancer Center and Research Institute**. You'll see billboards along I-85 showing real-time (typically five-minute) wait times for emergency room attention in its ER facility.

Patients at the Pelham Medical campus have access to primary physician care, medical and surgical specialties and full diagnostic capabilities, including imaging, a surgery center and rehabilitation. Just off Highway 14 in Greer, this state-of-the-art facility truly focuses on convenience to patients.

Arts & Entertainment

Greenville is a magnet for artists of all kinds. It's brimming with venues and enough tempting events to fill anyone's calendar more than twice over. There's way too much to do it all.

Live Music

Free, sponsored concerts are a big downtown draw the latter part of the week in warm weather months. Head to NOMA Square for Thursdays' Downtown Alive and Main Street Fridays; or the TD Stage next to the Peace Center for Saturday night Reedy River Concerts.

Hot Tip: NOMA = North Main. NOMA Square is the public space in front of the Hyatt on North Main Street.

Furman University hosts an incredibly popular outdoor concert series called **Music by the Lake.** Furman's amphitheater seating faces a gorgeous lake (right on the Swamp Rabbit Trail!) with a path all the way around it. Most amazing of all, the university's bell tower pipes each concert across the lake. **Faculty concerts** are also awesome, and they're free.

The **Peace Center** affords patrons a world-class acoustical setting and all sorts of tremendous **touring acts**, everything from Sheryl Crow to The Hot Sardines.

64

Hot Tip: Spring for an affordable 'Peacemaker' membership to get early dibs on tickets.

Adjacent to the Peace Center, the outdoor amphitheater (currently branded the **TD Stage**) has its own appealing lineup when it's nice out, including a popular **summer concert series**. A terraced lawn offers both grass and stone seating, but chairs are allowed, too.

One of the city's true treasures is the **Greenville Symphony Orchestra**, which compares favorably to orchestras in major metros. Beloved Boston Pops conductor **Keith Lockhart**, a Furman grad, also makes regular appearances as guest conductor. Practically the entire city turns out for the symphony's annual **Christmas spectacular**.

The **Greenville Little Theater** and **Centre Stage** also offer concerts and musical performances throughout the year.

West End String Band playing a local gig
Photo courtesy of Ken Voltz

Greenville has such an abundance of great touring acts, as well as free concerts, it's amazing so many smaller venues faithfully offer a steady stream of musical

65

talent. Top marks go to **Smiley's Acoustic Cafe; Moe Joe's Coffee, Rainer's Bar** and **The Poinsett Hotel lobby bar.** Also worth exploring are **Chicora Alley; Blues Boulevard; Southern Culture; Velo Fellow; Mac Arnold's; Nose Dive; Wild Wing Cafe; The Blind Horse Saloon;** and Greer's **Rhythm & Brews.**

Fountain Inn occasionally brings in some touring performers at its downtown **Younts Center for Performing Arts**, and offers popular **free downtown concerts** on Friday and Saturday nights in summer.

Here's a short list—from several different musical genres—of talented local performers who deliver a great musical experience: pianist **Eric Barnhart;** guitarist **Steve Watson;** vocal and guitar duo **Katie & Larry;** the **Craig Sorrels Project** for jazz; the **Kelly Jo Connect** band; **Soul Ripple** for old-school blues, funk, soul and rock; **The Carousers;** vocalist **Darby Wilcox;** and the **West End String Band**, for bluegrass. Keep an eye out, too, for performances by singer-songwriter **Edwin McCain:** Greenville's talented native son still occasionally treats us to a concert.

Hot Tip: Check the Fete Greenville app for local music listings.

Theater

The Peace Center (with its multiple stages) thrills fans by offering world-class Broadway shows, including Tony-award-winning plays and musicals, throughout the year. The Peace keeps its more intimate stages busy, too. Stay abreast of what's happening on its calendar of upcoming events. In summer months, the free theatrical productions dubbed **Shakespeare in the Park** are held on a dedicated stage near downtown's Falls.

The Warehouse Theater, in the West End, maintains a highly devoted fan base with its intimate setting and extremely high quality plays and musicals. Ticketholders are treated to everything from Chekhov dramas to holiday satire. Rocky Horror has made more than one titillating appearance and The Warehouse's annual fundraiser is one of the city's don't-miss soirees. River Street's worthwhile **Centre Stage** shakes things up by offering Main Stage Shows (comedy, drama, musicals); Fringe Series Shows (based on serious 'human experience' topics), its New Play Festival, and other special evenings.

66

Kinky Boots production at The Peace Center
Photo courtesy of The Peace Center, by Matthew Murphy

Greenville Little Theatre, on the Heritage Green campus, stages popular productions (from Scarface to Mary Poppins) but also crafts shows especially for young audiences. This, the Upstate's oldest local live theater, also produces a fast and funny "studio" series, after which its improv troupe keeps the smiles coming.

You'll get a kick out of the satirical **Cafe & Then Some** dinner theater productions which poke wonderful fun at high-profile people, situations and trending topics. Check local papers, downtown posters and social media for other **comedy** offerings.

Hot Tip: Your entertainment budget will mostly be spent in Greenville's relatively compact downtown, so study which parking garage will best suit your needs for each theater.

Greenville **Chautauqua** keeps history alive by presenting its one-man (or woman) presentations by nationally acclaimed historical presenters; try to catch a show, discussion or the June festival. The **Milltown Players** in nearby

67

Pelzer also offer up some highly entertaining theatrical productions in a fairly intimate setting. And you'll eventually want to visit the renowned **Flat Rock Playhouse** in the nearby North Carolina village of the same name.

Dance

Greenville's own **dance** troupes—**Carolina Ballet** and **International Ballet**—share the Peace Center calendar with some of the biggest names in dance and movement. Names like Stomp, Pilobolus, Martha Graham, The Joffrey…any or all could grace the boards of The Peace stage.

The real dance star in Greenville, however, is not a person, but a style. If someone with a twinkle in his or her eye asks you to **shag**, don't be embarrassed: it's the **state dance of South Carolina**. This lively swing-style dance, done most often to Carolina Beach Music, inspires shag nights, shag contests, shag lessons and all sorts of opportunities to make new footloose friends.

Dance Arts Greenville students enjoy learning together
Photo courtesy of Larissa Koffskey

Visual Arts

The mixed-use **RiverPlace** project, which sits along the Reedy, holds **below-market-rate studios** on its first level, keeping the city's creative energy front

68

and center. Greenville's downtown is also brimming with **public art**; the **Dale Chihuly** memorial statue 'Rose Crystal Tower,' gracing Harriett's Garden in Falls Park, is particularly lovely at night.

Local visual artists open their working studios to the public for a weekend during November's greatly anticipated **Greenville Open Studios**, a project of the **Metropolitan Arts Council (MAC)**. MAC-sponsored **First Fridays** bring out more residents and visitors on a monthly basis, when galleries stay open late. Beyond downtown's West End, the area branding itself as **The Village of West Greenville**, with a mix of galleries, retail and bars/restaurants, buzzes on First Friday evenings

Greenville Center for the Creative Arts (GCCA) is one of the entities taking advantage of a repurposed textile mill on the city's west side. The GCCA offers public art classes, studio space and exhibitions. A few art courses are also typically available at **OLLI (Osher Lifelong Learning Institute)**.

Among Greenville's best galleries are **Mary Praytor Gallery** on Main Street; **Bennett's Frame & Art Gallery** on Laurens Road; and **Hampton III** on Wade Hampton Boulevard.

Artisphere, ranked #3 Best Art Festival in USA TODAY 10BEST Reader's Choice Contest in 2015, has an annual attendance approaching 85,000; over 1,000 applicants vie for a coveted space in this inspiring downtown festival.

The entire Blue Ridge mountain region has a rich history of arts and crafts. Asheville, Black Mountain, Brevard and Maggie Valley, NC all make for great day trips, as will Southern Highland Craft Guild locations, and regional art festivals.

Outstanding Museums

To its great credit, Greenville is home to three outstanding art museums. The **Smithsonian-affiliated Greenville County Museum of Art**, on the Heritage Green campus, is home to the world's largest public collection of watercolors by iconic American artist Andrew Wyeth, and also holds an impressive number of Jasper Johns. The GCMA mounts a variety of intriguing exhibitions throughout the year, as well as concerts, talks and special events for benefactors.

Bob Jones' University's Museum & Gallery (M&G) happens to own one of the world's largest collections of European Old Master paintings in America, jaw-dropping canvases by van Dyck, Rubens, Tintoretto and many other masters of the 14th through 19th centuries. **M&G Heritage Green** rotates special collections of its works in its easy-to-reach satellite location on the cultural campus adjacent to downtown.

Higher Education & Continued Learning

Greenville's **Furman University** is considered one of the country's premier undergraduate liberal arts colleges. Six of ten grads are working in a business-related field. Furman also participates in NCAA Division I athletics. Furman's campus is legendary for its beauty, but cranks out many a success story.

Furman University's beautiful campus
Photo courtesy of GreenvilleRelocation.com

While **Clemson University**'s main campus is located 45 minutes west of Greenville in a small town of the same name, it has a tremendous presence and alumni community here. The university's **graduate business program** in the heart of the city gives students the opportunity to obtain a traditional MBA or study for a master's degree in entrepreneurship and innovation; marketing; management; professional accountancy; or real estate development.

70

Clemson University's International Center for Automotive Research (CU-ICAR), which parallels I-85, intends to be the premier automotive research, innovation and educational enterprise in the world. CU-ICAR's cutting-edge research emphasizes industry relevance and sustainability.

The opening of the four-year **University of South Carolina School of Medicine at Greenville Health System**'s main campus is another feather in the city's higher education cap. Students work side by side with GHS doctors in a hospital setting with the latest simulation, clinical and information technology.

With multiple campuses throughout the Upstate, **Greenville Technical College** has been giving its enrollees skill sets which are often relevant to Greenville's changing business environment: healthcare, technology, business, automotive and public service careers. Dr. Keith Miller, President, says "individuals can access education to advance their careers or change directions" at Greenville Tech.

Bob Jones University, a renowned Christian University, offers a wide range of disciplines in its undergrad and grad programs, while equipping students "with a biblical worldview and the ability to defend that worldview." The school is particularly strong in visual communications and also produces abundant numbers of respected CPAs.

University Center offers degrees from many colleges
Photo courtesy of GreenvilleRelocation.com

71

University Center Greenville (on south Pleasantburg) brings even more opportunity while adding to the academic vibe of the area. This city campus offers undergrad and grad programs from six partner universities: **Clemson, USC, USC Upstate, Furman, Anderson University** and **SC State University.**

Amazingly, Greenville is also home to over half a dozen **small colleges and universities,** where you can begin, continue or complete an education. Choose from Brown Mackie College, ECPI College of Technology, ITT Technical, Southern Wesleyan University, Strayer University, Virginia College or Webster University.

Continued Learning opportunities are world class in Greenville. The **Osher Lifelong Learning Institute (OLLI)** has its own dedicated building on the Furman campus, and offers a boggling variety of classes and trips throughout the year. You'll find OLLI's catalog online.

North Greenville University, located in the scenic foothills below Glassy Mountain and just minutes from Travelers Rest, is a coed liberal arts institution integrating academic discipline with the tenets of a Christian lifestyle. Nearby Spartanburg is home to both **Wofford College** and **Converse College,** while Anderson, SC (about 25 miles southwest of Greenville) is the site of highly-ranked **Anderson University,** also recognized for the tremendous value it offers.

*Hot Tip: If you're 60 or older, be sure to investigate the state's amazing **Plan 60** option, in which courses are free.*

72

CHAPTER 3: WHERE TO LIVE

Real Estate Overview

In a word, the Greenville market is hot. The city's wealth of awards—most of which have been widely publicized in national media—have buyers coming in from markets all over America (and more than a few from other countries). People are leaving behind over-priced, over-crowded cities for the comfort, affordability and lifestyle of the Upstate, and their money goes much further here. Another strong trend is the **average days on market**, which has seen a steady decrease since Greenville's rise in popularity: average days before sale has declined from 113 in 2011 to just 76 in 2015, according to the Greater Greenville Association of Realtors (GGAR).

When shopping for a home, you'll have more competition than you would have a few years ago, but there are still good values in Greenville.

Cost of Living

A large part of Greenville's appeal is its cost of living. The Greenville Area Development Council's website shows the latest cost of living figures from The Council for Community and Economic Research, which produces a trusted cost of living index for cities across the USA. A score below 100 indicates a city is less expensive than the average of all US cities. At last reporting—Q3 of 2015—Greenville's score was 93.8, **below the national average.**

Where You'll Pay the Most

As of early 2016, the demand for neighborhoods near downtown—whether established, transitioning or developing—had created a seller's market in a few established neighborhoods in the heart of the city. A seller's market can create or lead to a multi-offer environment, in which two or more potential buyers are competing for the same home. In that type of market, a seller may require a pre-approval letter before a bid is considered or accepted. Many Realtors

74

will also require a pre-approval letter or proof of funds before they show you properties. Either of those documents also helps your Realtor do a better job by focusing on price ranges in which you're qualified to purchase.

Hot Tip: If you're having trouble with pre-approval, a Realtor can put you in touch with a lender who can help.

There are a few luxury neighborhoods and communities scattered across town and in various parts of the county. Thornblade (on the eastside) is one of these, as are Cobblestone and Kingsbridge (to the south), and The Cliffs (to the north). Some luxury buyers are also opting for custom built homes on acreages.

Outdoor living space gets a lot of use in Greenville
Courtesy of Gabriel Builders, photo by T.J. Getz

Where the Values Are

Neighborhoods farther from downtown have felt far less impact in terms of price appreciation. The same $425,000 that buys a near-downtown Craftsman-style bungalow, with little closet space and no large rooms, will—when you go to Simpsonville—buy a spacious, new, two-story brick palace by comparison.

But you can spend half that, and still purchase a nice home in Greenville's Eastside, or in Greer, Taylors, Easley or Powdersville.

As of early 2016, the median price of homes and condos *listed for sale* was $229,000. Since a few higher-priced homes can skew a sales average, let's look at *median sale prices* of homes/condos in Greenville in recent years:

2015	$172,000
2014	$163,000
2013	$156,500
2012	$150,000
2011	$142,000

Average sale prices in the same years were about $30,000 higher.

Mortgage Pre-Qualification

If it's been a few years since you purchased your last home, post-recession mortgage demands are very different. You can anticipate having to provide much more documentation than you did before. The system is much stricter now; lending standards have tightened down.

What does this mean for buyers? It's very important to get pre-qualified because it's much tougher to get a mortgage than it was before the crash. **Having a local lender can be a real advantage**, particularly in a multi-offer situation when sellers lean toward the most efficient offer. It's also nice to be able to sit and talk with a local lender, or to be able to contact them easily if there are questions or challenges during the buying process.

Property Taxes

South Carolina does have one of the **lowest median property tax rates** in the United States. There's a **statewide property tax rate of 4%** for an owned home in which you live. (Rental homes and second homes are taxed at 6%).

In Greenville County, there are **several districts which levy additional taxes**. At the property tax office (County Square on University Ridge near downtown) they've gone to the trouble of creating a millage sheet for all the different districts of the county, showing the breakdown of taxes for each district, *including* the additional levies. You'll see millage rates for state, city, school, sewer, fire and any miscellaneous levies which have been voter-approved, and the total millage for each district. Property taxes and sale records can be found on the Greenville County Geographic Information Systems (GCGIS) website, but it's much easier to let your Realtor do the legwork for you.

South Carolina property taxes are computed on the fair market value of your home, minus any eligible exemptions. In South Carolina, people over 65 can apply for a $50,000 homestead exemption on any primary residence they occupy. The same application can be made by legally blind occupying homeowners, or anyone classified by Social Security as disabled. If granted, the exemption kicks in a full calendar year later. Veterans who are 100% disabled can apply for exemptions through the Department of Revenue. Homes are reassessed every five years in Greenville County. The sales price you pay can affect the fair market value of your home.

In 2015, taxes for owner-occupied homes in the city of Greenville were taxed at a millage rate of .3376, which means a $200,000 fair market value property could have cost $2700 per year in property taxes. Rates vary quite a bit across Greenville County: 2015 levies ranged from .2518 to .4160 millage (a difference which translates to about $1,314 per year, on a $200,000 home). Rates also vary from county to county: neighboring Pickens and Anderson Counties have historically taxed property owners at a lower rate than Greenville County.

PROPERTY TAX EXAMPLE:

$200,000 fair market value of the home
   x 4% assessment ratio
= $8,000 assessed value of the home
   x .323 millage rate per (323 mills per 1000)
= $2,584 taxes due

Hot Tip: *Keep in mind that the cost of living in Greenville County is still below the national average.*

77

Choosing a Realtor

It's important to choose well when deciding which Realtor to have represent you. **Greater Greenville Area Realtors** (GGAR) has a full list of all the licensed Realtors in the area, but a comprehensive list doesn't give you any clues as to who would best suit your needs. A **mortgage broker** is a wonderful source for a professional recommendation; each works with dozens of Realtors throughout the year, seeing which pros pay attention to details and please clients.

By following a recommendation, you can also be successfully paired with a Realtor who regularly manages sales in your price range and who's got **strength in the geographic areas that interest you**, or with whom you may have something in common.

Furnishing and Decorating your New Home

Greenville has a surprising wealth of resources when it comes to building materials, furnishings and all things design. One local designer has shared his go-to sources for practically everything you need to pull together a new home; you'll find those lifesavers on GreenvilleRelocation.com. Retailers and designers are charted in this book.

SEE ALSO: Getting Oriented: **Goods & Services / Furnishings, Design**

Communities, Towns and Neighborhoods

Where will you live? That's a big question, and the decisions you make will impact many facets of your life, from commutes to schools and everything in between.

If your primary concern is your **commute or proximity to a specific place**, then determine what major road your main "place of interest" (i.e. a new employer) is on or near, then keep reading. Outlying communities are labeled by commute corridor, another way to determine an area which will work for you. **Non-incorporated areas** give more freedom from zoning restrictions, certain laws and even some taxes, but you never know what might wind up next door.

If **lower real estate taxes** are important, then you might want to look at Anderson and Pickens County communities and neighborhoods. If **crime** is a concern, maps on the Neighborhood Scout website detail where it occurs; it tends to be highly concentrated.

Here's what's meant when you see these terms regarding housing prices:

- **Affordable:** 100K-300K
- **Midrange:** 300K-600K
- **High End:** Over 600K

Now it's time to dig into this multi-faceted topic.

Living within the **city of Greenville** gives you a fantastic lifestyle as well as some serious bragging rights. Greenville offers Falls Park, an amazing downtown, Cleveland Park, beautiful historic neighborhoods, diverse architectural styles, great options on dining and entertainment, and a small town feel, but with big city amenities.

	Greenville
Arts, Entertainment	✓
Golf Course Homes	✓
Historic Homes	✓
Incorporated	✓
Lakes	
Lower RE Taxes	
Mtn Views	✓
Parks / Greenspace	✓
Some Rural / Acreages	✓
Walkable downtown	✓
Near the airport (GSP)	✓
Near I-385 or I-85	✓
Near a hospital	✓

79

Greenville Areas

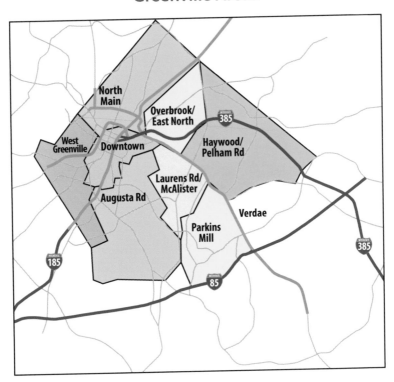

Popular Greenville Areas

Augusta Road: Augusta Road, which feeds into downtown, is midrange-to-high end and offers all conveniences, restaurants and small shops. Architectural styles are diverse and neighborhoods are gorgeous. Golf carts are a popular vehicle option. The Greenville Country Club is near here, and sister club Chanticleer is nearby.

Downtown: Downtown offers the urban lifestyle, in a mid-to-high price range: housing options include lofts, condos, townhomes, and single family homes. Adjacent neighborhoods Cleveland Forest, Alta Vista and Heritage Park offer gracious living and beautiful architectural styles; the historic Hampton Pinckney neighborhood is transitional and offers homes in all price ranges. You'll also find rentals, if you want to experience life downtown before purchasing here.

Haywood / Pelham lies just minutes from downtown via 385. While traffic can be bad at 5 p.m., home and condo prices are affordable to mid-range in this convenient area. Mountain views are possible in a few key places.

North Main: North Main is a welcoming, architecturally diverse area of mostly mid-to-high-end homes just minutes from downtown. The mid-to-high priced Stone Lake neighborhood is near the popular Stone Lake Community Club pool (get on the wait list if you're keen). The Dellwood and Chick Springs neighborhoods are popular with families and are more affordable.

Welcoming cottages are plentiful in Greenville
Photo courtesy of GreenvilleRelocation.com

Overbrook / East North: Historic Overbrook, near downtown, has midrange, easily affordable and transitional neighborhood homes. This area lies between Bob Jones University and 385 coming into downtown.

Parkins Mill: This gracious area near downtown spans the gamut on pricing, from affordable to over two million. Gower, popular with families, has low- to mid-range ranch homes and a community pool, and is near shopping.

Verdae: Popular Verdae is a relatively new, large master-planned community. Small yards, town squares, sidewalks, neighborhood shops and nice parks define this high-density mid-range to high-end neighborhood of homes and condos between Laurens and Woodruff Roads. The larger area is sometimes referred to as Paramount Park.

West Greenville: A former mill area, this affordable transitional area is home to the poppin' VIllage of West Greenville and a wide variety of housing, including in former mills. It lies just west of downtown Greenville.

81

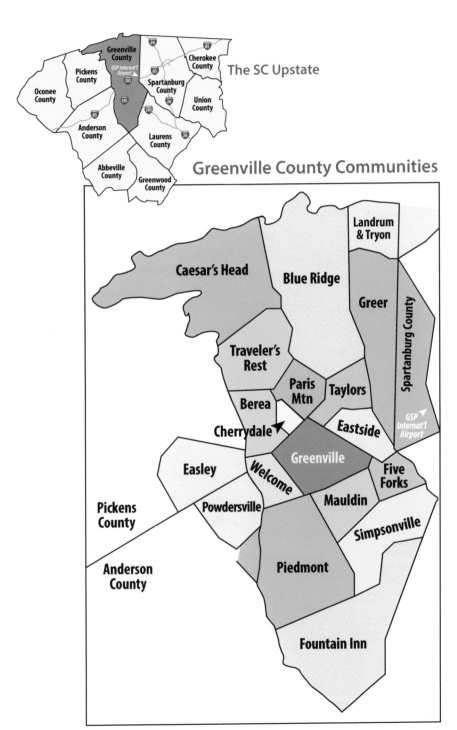

The SC Upstate

Greenville County Communities

Alternatives to the City of Greenville

Many places commonly associated with Greenville are actually just outside city limits and technically lie within Greer, Taylors or Travelers Rest. Others are incorporated cities or unincorporated areas, including in other counties. Here's a look at the places to live outside the city limits, and what each offers.

Blue Ridge: *NW of Greenville – Hwy 25 and 101 corridors*
Blue Ridge is truly a rural setting with rolling hills, big mountain views and lots of privacy. It's very low density but all the conveniences you'll need are a short drive away, in Greer, Taylors or Travelers Rest.

Caesars Head: *NW of Greenville – 276 corridor*
The somewhat exclusive Caesars Head neighborhood adjacent to Caesars Head State Park is most commonly associated with weekends and summer getaways, due to its mountaintop location. But the larger area offers lots of opportunity for affordable, private mountain living.

County	Greenville	Greenville	Pickens	Greenville
Direction from Greenville	N	NW	W	E
Community	**Blue Ridge**	**Caesars Head**	**Easley**	**Eastside**
Arts, Entertainment				
Golf Course Homes				
Historic Homes		✓		
Incorporated			✓	
Lakes		✓		
Lower RE Taxes			✓	
Mtn Views	✓	✓	✓	
Parks / Greenspace		✓		✓
Some Rural / Acreages	✓	✓	✓	
Walkable downtown			✓	
Near the airport (GSP)				✓
Near I-385 or I-85			✓	✓
Near a hospital				✓

Easley: *W of Greenville - Hwy 123 corridor*
This Pickens County city, to the west of Greenville, is blessed with urban conveniences while offering opportunities for rural life or views. To its north—toward the mountains—lie farms, countryside, and high points affording Blue Ridge Mountain vistas. Easley has a cute downtown (an active train rolls through) while its east side holds big-box stores. Stately traditional homes cost less than in Greenville, and the commute is quick and easy. Easley's not on an interstate, but is only 10-15 minutes from I-85.

Eastside: *E of Greenville - 29 / Wade Hampton and I-385 corridors*
The Eastside area is a magnet for families with kids and first-time buyers. Neighborhoods by the dozens offer homes in all sizes and styles, with big yards, and prices which offer a lot of bang for the buck. Eastside also has good schools. The trade-off: heavy traffic during rush hours.

Five Forks: *SE of Greenville - Woodruff Road corridor*
Five Forks is an unincorporated area about the same size as Mauldin and Simpsonville and lies just east of the I-385 / I-85 interchange. This popular area is fed by shopping artery Woodruff Road and gets its name from the confluence of roads which converge there, including Batesville Road. The Five Forks area is convenient to GE Energy, Michelin, BMW and GSP.

Fountain Inn: *SE of Greenville - 276 / Laurens Road corridor*
This tiny town to Greenville's east is about 20 minutes from downtown Greenville and not too far from GSP. It's reached via I-385, so the commute is easy. Fountain Inn's downtown—which has its own farmers market—has seen a remarkable revitalization in recent years, the perfect complement to an already stellar collection of historic homes. This inviting burg is also home to Fountain Inn Civic Center, which hosts traveling shows and performers. Real estate prices are affordable, and nearby is major employer Walmart Distribution Center. You'll love Fountain Inn's free downtown concerts and annual Christmas festival, and the way its historic homes are decorated.

84

County	Greenville	Greenville	Greenville	Greenville
Direction from Greenville	E	SE	NE	SE
Community	**Five Forks**	**Fountain Inn**	**Greer**	**Mauldin**
Arts, Entertainment		✓	✓	
Golf Course Homes			✓	
Historic Homes		✓	✓	
Incorporated		✓	✓	✓
Lakes				
Lower RE Taxes				
Mtn Views			✓	
Parks / Greenspace		✓	✓	✓
Some Rural / Acreages	✓	✓	✓	
Walkable downtown		✓	✓	
Near the airport (GSP)	✓		✓	✓
Near I-385 or I-85	✓	✓	✓	✓
Near a hospital	✓	✓	✓	✓

Greer: *NE of Greenville - 29 / Wade Hampton corridor*
Greer, to Greenville's northeast, is a hotspot in full growth mode. The city lies mainly between the commercial artery of Hwy 29 (aka Wade Hampton Road) and I-85 North, but a few incorporated parts stretch northward along the South Tyger River and Lake Robinson. Greer is large: annexed portions of the city also stretch down Highway 14 toward Simpsonville. Major landmarks which share a Greer address include GSP airport, Greenville's Inland Port and BMW Manufacturing. You'll find a wide variety of housing and price points here. Greer's downtown has great bones and lots of potential. Highways 101 and 14 both bisect Greer, making commutes easy. Downtown Greenville is 15-30 minutes away.

Mauldin: *SE of Greenville - 276 / Laurens Road corridor*
The small city of Mauldin lies along I-385 just to the south of Greenville. Its high point is proximity to Conestee Park, a huge recreational campus with a dog park, hiking trails and sports opportunities. Mauldin offers extremely affordable housing and is close to Greenville's Millennium campus, CU-ICAR and Greenville

85

Tech. Mauldin ties into Greenville's south Laurens and Pleasantburg Roads, and is bisected by Butler and Miller Roads, all of which lead to major shopping areas and the freeways. SC-TAC is minutes away from the city's western edge.

To see pictures of all communities, go to **GreenvilleRelocation.com**.

Paris Mountain: *N of Greenville - Hwy 25 corridor*
Homes on Paris vary from the exclusive, expensive estates with huge views (and much colder weather, at higher elevations) to affordable homes at its base. You'll find condos and mid- to high-range foothill homes inside the Montebello neighborhood. Paris Mountain State Park is a Mecca for hikers, cyclists and outdoor lovers of all kinds.

Piedmont: *S of Greenville - Hwy 25 corridor*
Tiny, rural Piedmont—straddling the Saluda River, southwest of Greenville—will appeal to folks who want privacy and space at a very affordable price. Piedmont lies in both **Greenville and Anderson Counties,** the Anderson side offering lower property taxes. The I-185 loop, practically devoid of cars, offers a speedy toll route from Piedmont to Mauldin, Simpsonville and I-385. Piedmont Highway provides a mostly rural drive into the heart of Greenville, while Anderson, SC and Anderson University lie just minutes to the southwest. Piedmont is also close to one of the Upstate's Michelin tire manufacturing facilities.

County	Greenville	Greenville	Anderson, Pickens
Direction from Greenville	N	SW	SW
Community	**Paris Mountain**	**Piedmont**	**Powdersville**
Arts, Entertainment			
Golf Course Homes		✓	
Historic Homes			
Incorporated			
Lakes			
Lower RE Taxes			✓
Mtn Views	✓	✓	✓
Parks / Greenspace	✓		
Some Rural / Acreages			✓
Walkable downtown		✓	

86

County	Greenville	Greenville	Anderson, Pickens
Direction from Greenville	N	SW	SW
Community	Paris Mountain	Piedmont	Powdersville
Near the airport (GSP)			✓
Near I-385 or I-85		✓	✓
Near a hospital			✓

Powdersville: *W of Greenville - Hwy 123 corridor*

Practically a "secret" community, much of unincorporated Powdersville gives homeowners the benefit of Anderson County real estate taxes while sited just 10-15 minutes from downtown Greenville. Many folks don't have a clue where Powdersville is, but longtime Greenville residents take pride in knowing about this area that's southwest of the city. Powdersville has no downtown, but affords all the primary conveniences, and Easley's big-box stores are minutes away. There are also many highly affordable opportunities for mountain and sunset vistas in the pretty, rolling land which makes up Powdersville; if you look at rural land, just be aware there's no zoning. Exit 39 from I-85 takes you home, as does Anderson Road, from the Fluor Field area of downtown Greenville.

The other twist to Powdersville is the **school situation.** You'll see, on the charts in the Schools chapter, that some Powdersville schools have Greenville addresses but are actually in an Anderson County district. If considering Powdersville for a location, be very aware that some Anderson District 1 schools have Greenville or Easley addresses. Be sure to tell your Realtor the school district of your choice.

Simpsonville: *SE of Greenville - 276 / Laurens Road corridor*

Popular Simpsonville has put effort into revitalizing its downtown, and it shows. You'll find a farmer's market here, as well as a smattering of appealing shops and restaurants. The city has a wide variety of home styles at all price points, and you get a *lot* for your money here. Commuting to Greenville or major employers is easy: I-385 bisects the city as does Highway 14. Many of the major big box stores can be found on Fairview Road, which also leads to bucolic countryside. Simpsonville's vastly appealing Heritage Park is a real draw for families and outdoor enthusiasts. Greenville Health System has a campus in Simpsonville, as does Greenville Technical College.

87

County	Greenville	Greenville	Greenville
Direction from Greenville	SE	N	NW
Community	Simpsonville	Taylors	Travelers Rest
Arts, Entertainment			✓
Golf Course Homes	✓	✓	✓
Historic Homes		✓	✓
Incorporated	✓		✓
Lakes		✓	
Lower RE Taxes			
Mtn Views		✓	✓
Parks / Greenspace	✓	✓	✓
Some Rural / Acreages	✓	✓	✓
Walkable downtown	✓		✓
Near the airport (GSP)	✓	✓	
Near I-385 or I-85	✓		
Near a hospital	✓		✓

Taylors: *NE of Greenville - 29 / Wade Hampton corridor*
Greenville's largest suburb is unincorporated and is often chosen by homeowners who want a little more space and a little less traffic, while being near the city. The sprawling Pebble Creek golf community lies in Taylors' northwest corner, less than a mile from Paris Mountain State Park. One of the area's redevelopment projects—Taylors Mill, along the Enoree River—offers potential as a hub for the area's revitalization. Taylors is bisected by busy Wade Hampton Road, which offers many shopping and dining opportunities, and affords a quick trip to downtown Greenville or Greer. Check out the Taylors Town Square website for updates on cool initiatives, or to get involved.

Travelers Rest: *N of Greenville - Hwy 25 corridor*
Named for its role as a stagecoach stop on the way to the mountains from the coast during hot summers, T.R. (as it's affectionately known) is enjoying a huge surge in popularity. Incorporated T.R. takes full advantage of the Swamp Rabbit Trail, which arrives there from Greenville after passing through Furman's campus. Downtown is a destination, with appealing restaurants, bars, shops

and outfitters. Residents of family-friendly neighborhoods near Furman have a quick hop into Greenville. Furman's campus offers continued learning and multiple recreational options, including public golf and tennis, college football and lakeside trails.

Travelers Rest (a.k.a. "T.R.") lies on the Swamp Rabbit Trail
Photo courtesy of GreenvilleRelocation.com

Unincorporated T.R. stretches all the way north to scenic Highway 11; acreages and farms in this hilly area have mountain views, as do a few key spots closer to town. Greenville Hospital System has a presence here and Greenville Tech's northwest campus and North Greenville University are both close by. The Cliffs' newest luxury golf community is sited at T.R.'s northern edge; just below the North Carolina state line.

You'll also find **Berea**, **Cherrydale** and **Welcome** on the Greenville county map. Housing is very affordable in these areas, all of which are close to downtown. Foodies might trek to Berea for *panaderias* and *carnecerias*, while residents of north Greenville neighborhoods regularly head to Pleasantburg Road in

89

Cherrydale for shopping and dining. This area, the gateway to Paris Mountain and T.R., also holds some newly constructed condo developments. Berea and Welcome both offer quick access to freeways.

Golf and Tennis Communities

Greenville is home to the pricey but gorgeous **Greenville Country Club (GCC)** and **Chanticleer**, which are affiliated. GCC sits atop one of the highest points in the city and has a very active tennis program. Commonly associated with Greenville but actually located in **Greer** is **Thornblade** community, with its Fazio course and another active tennis community. The sprawling **Pebble Creek** community has a **Taylors** address; its two courses are complemented by an active tennis program. **Easley** holds **Smithfields** residential golf course community.

Simpsonville is home to popular **Holly Tree** (Plantation), which has many, many golf and tennis players in residence and enjoying its course and tennis program. (It also has a golf academy). In **Travelers Rest** lies **Green Valley**, while in the mountain foothills but still with a T.R. address are **Cherokee Valley** (huge golf course views and tennis courts); and the exclusive luxury communities of **The Cliffs**, its seven courses designed by the greats, and a bevy of pros managing the members' golf and tennis programs. **Paris Mountain Country Club** has nearby neighborhoods which are unaffiliated.

Photo courtesy of GreenvilleRelocation.com

90

Communities with Amenities

If you're not a golfer, but you like lots of amenities in your neighborhood—clubhouse, pool, sports areas, walking trails and more—you might want to consider the area's many planned communities, lovely places like **Acadia** and **Spaulding Farm**, which offer some, if not all, of the extras on your wish list. The family-friendly city of **Simpsonville** is loaded with neighborhoods like this, but there are several in other communities as well.

Hot Tip: RealEstateScorecard.com gives scores to master planned communities throughout the Southeast.

Retirement Communities

The friendly and affordable 55+ **Swansgate** neighborhood, near downtown and two hospitals, offers affordable patio homes and condos just moments from tony Augusta Road shopping. Swansgate has a clubhouse, pool, gym, a pond and stream, and its own tennis court.

Greenville has two high-end campuses for those who want to enjoy their senior years in comfort, convenience and surrounded by a more active population. The well-heeled residents at **Cascades Verdae**, sited between Laurens and Woodruff Roads, enjoy elegant housing and clubhouse facilities, along with a full slate of activities, and transportation to local cultural events. Residents have the option of independent or assisted living, and Cascades also offers continuing care, skilled nursing, rehabilitation and memory care.

The Woodlands at Furman, with its upscale apartments located a few minutes north of downtown, also offers many of the same options, and has an ace up its sleeve. The adjacent Furman University campus offers residents a beautiful environment which is also stimulating. The Woodlands has independent and assisted living, memory care and skilled nursing.

On Greenville's eastside, the sprawling **Rolling Green Village** sits atop 175 gently rolling acres and offers continuing care for residents of its affordable apartments and patio homes. This community's Health Center gives residents options that include rehab therapy, skilled nursing, assisted living, respite and memory care; it's also conveniently located near lots of eastside shopping.

Greenville Area Schools

The Greenville County Schools (GCS) system has many strengths and some exceptional schools. The Upstate also offers the option of some wonderful private schools. Recognized as a nationally-accredited school system of excellence, GCS offers education in every type of setting and leads the state in school choice. A full 15% of students attend a school of choice, rather than simply attending the one closest to home. You too, will be able to find a great fit for your children's needs as well as their passions. Despite its size (46th in the nation), the GCS system bested the national average ACT score in 2015.

The bulk of this chapter is regarding schools in **Greenville County**, although reference is made to a few select schools in nearby counties offering lower property taxes. The chapter is arranged in a way that will give you a starting point for dialogue and further research.

*Hot Tip: At the end of this chapter, you'll find **time-saving charts** detailing area schools, including district and location, grades served, some web-based rankings, charter or magnet status, and any church affiliations.*

Now let's dive into some specific areas of interest and study.

Arts

Greenville is actually one of the most inspiring cities in the southeast for arts-oriented students and families. The **South Carolina Governor's School for the Arts and Humanities**, a resident high school adjacent to downtown's Falls Park, is cranking out true performance stars. Before their names go up in lights, students live, study and perform in Greenville.

Your kids don't have to attend the Governor's School to take advantage of the area's penchant for the arts, however. Students who excel in the arts have the opportunity to apply for a spot at the Greenville School District's **Fine Arts Center**, on the **Wade Hampton High School campus**. Areas of discipline include

92

architecture, creative writing, dance, digital filmmaking, music (instrumental and voice), theater and visual arts. The staff includes professionals acclaimed in their fields; students are selected on the basis of talent, but also on their levels of interest, motivation and commitment.

Greenville County Schools
Greenville, SC   *www.greenville.k12.sc.us*

101 schools & centers

99% of teachers are **Highly Qualified.** **100%** are fully certified.

72,712 Students

888,042 Volunteer Hours

9,506 employees

School Report Cards

97.7% of schools earned ratings of Excellent, Good or Average on their School Report Card.

22.0 Our students' **average** ACT College Entrance Test score of 22.0 exceeds the state (20.4) and national (21.0) averages.

State's Largest **School Choice** Program

15% of students (10,000) attend on **Choice.**

AA+ Aa1 GCS received the highest credit ratings possible for SC school districts: AA+ by Standard & Poor's and Aa1 by Moody's.

April 2015

93

Stone Academy elementary school offers its students a dance studio, drama room, band room, and dedicated spaces for strings and piano. Its Arts Alive festival brings in guest artists and the school integrates arts across its curriculum. Drama and dance are taught weekly.

Eastside High in Taylors has two Art Studios, and a Kiln Room. And Piedmont's **Woodmont High School** is a regular participant (and winner) in the SC Theatre Association High School Play Festival.

Gifted and International Baccalaureate (IB)

GCS offers a full range of K-12 IB continuum: Primary Years, Middle Years, and Diploma. The students in your family can join the IB sequence without screening or testing, in any one of four different geographical areas. All but two of the county's IB schools serve the kids directly in the vicinity. (The exceptions are Beck Middle Academy and Southside High).

Greenville's IB schools are spread across the county. **Elementary schools** with IB programs are Chandler Creek (NE), Fork Shoals (S), Heritage (NW) and Sara Collins (central). The area's **middle schools** with IB programs are Greer (NE), Northwest (NW), Woodmont (S) and Beck Academy (central).

IB high schools are Greer (NE), Southside (central), Travelers Rest (NW) and Woodmont (southern). Woodmont's IB Diploma Program offers an impressive 21 courses for juniors and seniors. The school has a full-time IB/AP Coordinator and 39 teachers trained in IB/AP.

Health Sciences

Carolina High School & Academy offers students a nationally certified 'Project Lead the Way' health program; a health sciences lab; a Health Magnet program; and its Health Occupation Students of America Program.

Language & Multi-Culture

As of this writing, **Blythe Academy** (K-5) is currently recognized as the state's only elementary school offering all students daily foreign language instruction

94

through either a FLES (Foreign Language in the Elementary School) or Partial Spanish or French Immersion program. The Academy's partial immersion students even receive math, science and health instruction in Spanish or French in some grades.

Middle school **League Academy of Communication Arts**, near North Pleasantburg Road, is a magnet school with a communication arts focus. Its Gifted and Talented Language Program puts students on the path to a bilingual career, and the school's partnership with the Peace Center performance hall is designed for staff development. LACA has a video production studio, three computer labs, and was the first school in the county to be named a "National School to Watch."

At **Langston Charter Middle School** on Woodruff Road, all students take Spanish every day, positioning them for multicultural career opportunities.

Beck Academy Middle School, an International Baccalaureate magnet school, says its mission is "to meet the academic needs of our culturally diverse student body in a safe environment that nurtures, accepts and encourages all students to be productive citizens of the global community, life-long learners and future leaders."

Greenville Middle Academy of Global and Traditional Studies
This newly constructed magnet school awards high school credit for Honors English I, Spanish I, French I, and French II. It has a French Immersion Program, and a Latin/Greek Vocabulary Development Program. It also offers College Board pre-advanced placement programs in English language arts.

*Hot Tip: Area special schools allow kids to learn in their native languages. These schools include Michelin **French** School, **Chinese** Saturday School, **Korean** Saturday School, **Japanese** Saturday School and **German** Saturday School.*

Media & Communications

Communications skills are critical to today's success. If you have a student at home who's interested in content production or strategy, or who seems to have a passion for writing or constructive social media, Greenville schools can offer them a winning path forward.

Students at **Stone Academy** (K-5, in the North Main neighborhood) enjoy the school's digital broadcast system that features a live student-centered program called Jumpstart News.

Dr. Phinnize J. Fisher Middle's Academic Related Arts Program includes creative writing, speech and drama, public speaking, broadcast journalism and newspapers. Its library is largely digital, and the school has a Gifted and Talented program.

Carolina High School & Academy (in SW Greenville) offers students unique broadcasting opportunities with its own live morning news show.

Greenville High School has its own production lab for broadcast journalism as well as web design and digital media classes, virtual enterprise classes and digital media lab.

A.J. Whittenberg Elementary
Photo courtesy of D.J. Henson

Science, Technology, Engineering and Math

If your child is interested in technology or engineering, you've struck gold. South Carolina's first elementary school with a school-wide engineering curriculum is **A.J. Whittenberg Elementary**, which offers LEGO Robotics. Second graders are

96

issued a tablet, and the school partners with influential local corporations and institutions, including Michelin, Fluor, GE Energy, Clemson University-ICAR and Hubbell Light, giving eye-opening ties to assignments and careers which are relevant. AJW is downtown.

East North Street Academy of Mathematics and Science (K-4)
Named an 'Outstanding Magnet School of Math and Science, East North partners with Michelin. It has a Gifted and Talented program; science/math labs weekly for all students; a Michelin Challenge Math Gifted Club; math/reading coaches; and 2nd, 3rd, 4th, 5th grade before-school Michelin Competitive Math Clubs.

Greenville Early College (6-9) implements the New Tech Network model and Carnegie Math curriculum. It has a University Partnership with Clemson, Furman & USC-Upstate and offers a Rising 6th grade week-long transition summer day camp at Furman

Dr. Phinnize J. Fisher Middle School, on Greenville's high-tech CU- ICAR campus, partners with neighboring Clemson. It's one of the county's newest schools and offers students a science, technology, engineering, arts, and math (STEAM) focused curriculum.

Fun Fact: This outstanding middle school was awarded a national recognition for design innovation and is being used as a model for schools across the country.

Sevier Middle, northeast of downtown, serves up an Engineering Design Program with Design & 3D Modeling; Robotics & Automation; Green Architecture; Energy & the Environment; STEM Career Simulation and Google 1st Computer Science Club. School updates are shared via Facebook, Instagram, Twitter, website and phone. (Sevier also has an outdoor garden, which is a pretty cool thing for families interested in sustainability).

Langston Charter Middle School, on Woodruff Road, also offers LEGO Robotics and junior forensics, perfect for any budding NCIS pros. (Langston students also wowed in 2013 by contributing 28,000 hours of community service).

Hughes Academy of Science and Technology (6-8) is a magnet school. Students have made the Elite Eight for Battle of the Brains in 2015, Final Four in

97

2014 and 2013. Hughes has a Dream Connectors Career Exploration Partnership with BMW, Michelin, and Greenville Health System and a TECHFIT (Teaching Engineering Concepts to Harness Future Innovators and Technologists) after-school program.

Carolina High School and Academy of Engineering Technology and Health Professions, on the city's southwest side, offers students an engineering lab and workshop with 3D Printers, a nationally certified 'Project Lead the Way' Engineering program and an engineering magnet program. It has produced Science Olympiad Award winners. Carolina HS implements the New Tech Network model for ALL 9th and 10th graders.

Greenville High School, near downtown, boasts a nationally certified Project Lead the Way program and Robotic team. This historic school has a rich history in Greenville and has the largest magnet program in the county, with a focus on courses in finance, business and law. A magnet Advisory Board is made up of community and school members.

Greenville Technical Charter High School, on the Greenville Tech campus between downtown and I-85, was recognized by US News and World Report as one of America's Top High Schools in 2015. Outfitted with new technology, this charter school appropriately aligns its curriculum to higher ed; students graduate with a semester of college under their belt. 2015 grads were awarded a cumulative total of $6,500,000 in scholarships, and an impressive 97% of all students go on to two- or four-year college.

J.L. Mann High School Academy of Mathematics, Science and Technology, near Laurens Road and I-85, has a robotics team, a United Way/Women in Engineering Partnership, and new technology in its classrooms. This school offers the New Tech Network model as an opt-in program. At over 1,700 students, it's a big school but offers advantages to STEM-oriented students.

Woodmont High School urges its students to apply for the annual scholarship challenge at The Mercer University School of Engineering in Macon, Georgia.

Greenville HS ladies tennis team
Photo courtesy of Stacey Krall

Special Needs

The Meyer Center (K-5), is a Charter School that's part of the Greenville School District. It focuses on education and therapy for children with medical challenges and disabilities. Students at this special school have the benefit of speech and language pathologists, physical therapists, occupational therapists, social workers and teachers who understand their special needs, all helping them to achieve their maximum potential.

The Washington Center, one of the only stand-alone special needs facilities in the state, is the District's facility for serving students K5-12 with significant physical delays.

Hidden Treasure Christian School has been helping kids with mental, physical, emotional and developmental disabilities since 1978. Part of Faith Baptist Church, this school has teachers who specialize in Asperger's Syndrome, autism, ADD/ADHD, dyslexia, giftedness and other disorders.

Charter Schools within Greenville County Schools

Greenville is home to seven charter schools. They're organized by lower, middle and high.

Lower Grades

• **Legacy Charter** (5K-4) Based on health and wellness including opportunities for 45 minutes of PE daily and healthy food options

Middle Grades

• **Langston Charter** (6-8) Based on a rigorous single-gender educational environment with a focus on leadership instruction and participation in community service activities
• **League Academy Charter** (6-8) Magnet program with communication arts focus and high school credit (Carnegie Units) for honors classes
• **Legacy Charter Middle** (5-8) Based on health and wellness including opportunities for dual college enrollment

Upper Grades

• **Brashier Middle College** (9-12) Goal of "College for Everyone"
• **Greenville Tech Charter HS** (9-12) Based on the focus of dual enrollment and alignment of HS & college curriculum; goal of students completing at least one semester of college work before graduation
• **Greer Middle College** (9-12) Dual-credit opportunities through our partnership with Greenville Technical College
• **Legacy Charter Early College** HS (9-12) In partnership with Greenville Technical College and North Greenville University; curriculum collaboration with Furman and Clemson Universities and Wofford College

Charter Schools within SC Charter School District

• **Quest Leadership Academy** (K4-3, with extra grade being added yearly through 2020) Based on the seven E's of Excellence in Education: Environment, Expectations, Encouragement, Excitement, Exposure,

Engagement and Experience.

• **GREEN Charter School** (K-9) Enriched math and science; students also develop an understanding of environmental sustainability, renewable energy, and technology. GREEN is not part of the Greenville County School District; it's funded by the state. GREEN capped its inaugural year (2013/14) with an Excellent rating on its state report card.

• **Lead Academy Public Charter School** (K5-8) - Four main values: be nice; work hard; serve well; have fun. "Just Do It" components focus on actionable items to build a strong community culture. Some fine arts and athletics are offered.

• **NEXT High School** is part of the innovative NEXT program (owned and funded subsidiary of the Greenville Chamber of Commerce) and teaches principles of innovation, design and entrepreneurship in a unique environment, utilizing the i3™ process of impact-based learning. Google Classroom is part of the mix at NEXT High School.

On the Greenville County Schools website, you'll find full descriptions of every public school. Just click on 'School Profile' to read more details.

Magnet Schools

The city of Greenville is home to nine of the district's eleven magnet academies, including one of the first elementary schools in the country to offer a school-wide engineering curriculum (A.J. Whittenberg Elementary). Here's a handy list which spells out the Greenville County magnet schools, as well as their specialties.

Beck Academy, International Baccalaureate Middle Years Program
Blythe Academy of Languages
Carolina HS and Academy of Engineering Technology and Health Professions
East North Street Academy of Mathematics and Science
Greenville Middle Academy of Global and Traditional Studies
Greenville High, Academy of Law, Finance and Business
Hughes Academy of Science and Technology
J. L. Mann High School Academy of Mathematics, Science and Technology

101

League Academy of Communication Arts
Southside High Intl. Baccalaureate Middle Years and Diploma Programs
Stone Academy of Communication Arts

Private Schools

Greenville is home to highly accredited private schools (K-3 to high school); there are nearly 60 of them in total. According to the stats at PrivateSchoolReview, over 10,000 students are enrolled in schools outside the school district program; the average cost for elementary tuition is $6,447; minorities make up 15% of the student body; the student teacher ratio is 12:1; and 83% of these schools are religiously affiliated (most of them Christian, many of them Baptist).

The list of private schools includes popular Southside Christian, Shannon Forest Christian (eastside), Bob Jones Academy, and Christ Church Episcopal. You'll find an important point to consider in these comments from one local mom, whose children have been attending Christ Church.

"My take on schools in Greenville," says mom Crimora Carter, "is we have a lot of solid alternatives: private, public, magnet…a ton of very positive choices for families," she says. "We ended up going the private school route. The smaller class sizes have been great for the kids."

The big issue for Carter was worries about the transition from lower school to middle school. "Making that transition on the same campus has been wonderful," she says. "No stress at all. There's that larger sense of community."

Career Centers

The school district also has four **Career Centers**, serving students in the 10th-12th grades. Three are located in Greenville; one is in Greer. Programs at these vocational learning hubs ready students for careers in fields that are highly relevant locally, including aircraft maintenance, automotive technology, digital art and design, and culinary arts. Students can also study barbering, cosmetology or nail technology; fashion design; law enforcement; or welding. Job shadowing, work-based learning and dual credits with Greenville Tech are advantages students are afforded.

Public Pre-K, Kindergarten & Elementary Schools						
Grades	School Name	Location	School District if other than GVL	Great Schools Rating	N'Hood Scout Rating vs US Schools	Charter or Magnet
K-5	Buena Vista	Greer		10	9	
PK-8	Sterling School	GVL		10	9	
PK-5	Oakview	Simp		10	9	
PK-5	Monarch	Simp		10	9	
PK-5	Skyland	Greer		9	9	
PK-5	Woodland	Greer		9	8	
PK-4	A.J. Whittenburg	GVL		9	9	
K-5	Pelham Road	GVL		9	8	
3-5	Powdersville	GVL	Anderson One	9	8	
1-5	Bethel	Simp		9	8	
1-5	Plain	Simp		9	8	
1-5	Rudolph Gordon	Simp		9	8	
PK-5	Brushy Creek	Taylors		9	8	
PK-5	Wren Elementary	Pdmnt	Anderson One	9	8	
PK-5	Crosswell	Easley	Pickens	8	6	
PK-5	East End	Easley	Pickens	8	7	
PK-5	Forest Acres	Easley	Pickens	8	7	
K-5	Augusta Circle	GVL		8	8	
PK-5	Blythe Academy	GVL		8	7	M
PK-5	Stone Academy	GVL		8	8	M
PK-5	Spearman	Pdmnt	Anderson One	8	8	
K-5	Bell's Crossing	Simp		8	7	
K-5	Bryson	Simp		8	7	
PK-5	Mountain View	Taylors		8	7	
PK-5	Brook Glenn	Taylors		8	7	
K-5	Paris	Taylors		8	8	
PK-5	Hunt Meadows	Easley	Anderson One	8	7	
K-5	Crestview	Greer		7	7	
PK-5	Mitchell Road	GVL		7	7	
K-5	Sara Collins	GVL		7	7	
PK-5	Simpsonville	Simp		7	7	

			Public Middle Schools			
Grades	School Name	Location	School District if other than GVL	Great Schools Rating	N'Hood Scout Rating vs US Schools	Charter or Magnet
M	Langston Charter	GVL		10	9	C
M	Sterling School	GVL		10	9	
M	Powdersville	GVL	Anderson One	9	7	
M	Riverside	Greer		9	8	
M	Greenville Middle Ac	GVL		9	7	M
M	League Academy	GVL		9	6	M
M	Blue Ridge	Greer		8	6	
M	Lead Academy Charter	GVL	SC Charter School	8	6	C
M	Beck Academy	GVL		8	5	M
M	Mauldin	Mauldin		8	5	
M	Ralph Chandler	Simp		8	5	
M	Northwood	Taylors		8	5	
M	Phinnize Fisher	GVL		NA	NA	
M	Greenville Early College	GVL		NA	NA	
M	Woodmont Middle	Pdmnt		NA	4	
M	Wren Middle	Pdmnt	Anderson One	9	7	
M	GREEN Charter	GVL	SC Charter School	9	NA	C

			Public High Schools			
Grades	School Name	Location	School District if other than GVL	Great Schools Rating	N'Hood Scout Rating vs US Schools	Charter or Magnet
M	NEXT High School	GVL	SC Charter School	NA	NA	C
M	Greenville Tech Charter	GVL		9	7	C
M	Brashier Middle College	Simp		9	7	C
M	Greer Middle College HS	Greer		8	8	C
M	Riverside HS	Greer		8	6	
M	Wren HS	Pdmnt	Anderson One	8	7	
M	Powdersville HS	GVL	Anderson One	8	7	
M	Wade Hampton HS	GVL		7	5	
M	Mauldin HS	Mauldin		7	6	
M	JL Mann Academy	GVL		6	5	
M	Hillcrest HS	Simp		6	6	
M	Governor's School of Arts	GVL	State	NA	NA	

104

			Private Schools		
P	K	Grades	School	Location	Church affiliated
*	*	PK-3	Montessori School Of Mauldin	Mauldin	
	*	1-12	Greenville Classical Academy	5 Forks	
*	*	1-2	Haynsworth School	GVL	
*	*	1-3	Montessori School Of Greenville	GVL	
*	*	1-4	First Presbyterian Academy	GVL	*
*	*	1-5	Abiding Peace Academy	Simp	*
*	*	1-5	Bethel Christian Academy	GVL	*
*	*	1-5	Bethlehem Christian Academy	Simp	*
*	*	1-5	Mitchell Road Christian Academy	GVL	*
	*	1-5	Carolina Intl. Prep School	GVL	
*	*	1-5	Hope Academy	GVL	
*	*	1-5	Palmetto Prep	GVL	
*	*	1-5	Bob Jones Elementary School	GVL	*
*	*	1-6	Sonrise Christian Academy	GVL	*
*	*	1-6	St Anthony Of Padua	GVL	*Catholic
*	*	1-6	Mt Zion Christian School	GVL	*
*	*	1-8	Our Lady Of The Rosary	GVL	*Catholic
	*	1-8	Paris Mountain Christian School	GVL	*
*	*	1-8	Upstate Christian Academy	GVL	*
*	*	1-8	Five Oaks Academy Montessori	Simp	
	*	1-8	The Chandler School	GVL	
		1-8	Camperdown Academy	GVL	
*	*	1-11	Piedmont Christian Academy	Pdmnt	*
		1-11	Word of Life Ministries	Simp	*
	*	1-12	Abundant Life Christian School	GVL	*
*	*	1-12	Bob Jones Academy	GVL	*
		1-12	Christ Church Episcopal School	GVL	*
*	*	1-12	E Georgia Rd Baptist Church	Simp	*
*	*	1-12	Fountain Inn Christian School	Ftn Inn	*
	*	1-12	Greenville Classical Academy	Simp	*
*	*	1-12	Hampton Park Christian School	GVL	*
*	*	1-12	Shannon Forest Christian School	GVL	*
*	*	1-12	Southside Christian School	Simp	*
	*	1-12	Tabernacle Christian School	GVL	*
		6-12	St Joseph's Catholic School	GVL	*Catholic
		6-12	Trinity Christian Academy	Pdmnt	*
		7-8	Bob Jones Junior High School	GVL	*

CHAPTER 4:
THE GREENVILLE LIFESTYLE

Festivals, Holidays & Special Events

Artisphere – May
This inspiring free festival includes artist demonstrations; four performing arts stages; Kidsphere area; and a Culinary Arts Café. South Main Street is alive with muralists, live statues, roving musicians and artists' booths.

Gallabrae and Greenville Scottish Games at Furman – May
The Great Scot Parade kicks off this festive weekend. Highland games on the field at Furman are but one component; there's also Celtic music, border collies, a British car show, a Scottish happy hour, a pageant, and Wee Scotland.

Fun Facts: When HRH The Prince Edward came to this event in 2010, it was the first time a member of the Royal Family had attended a Scottish games outside of Scotland. Greenville is located within one of the highest concentrations of Scots-Irish descendants in the USA.

Greek Festival – May
Food, music, coffee and cultural tours are all offered in abundance at this popular spring event hosted by St. George Greek Orthodox Cathedral.

Red White and Blue Festival – July
As one of the largest fireworks displays in South Carolina, the celebration features live music, food and a variety of family activities. The event happens downtown on several streets, which are blocked off to motor traffic.

Euphoria – September
Greenville's renowned Euphoria is a decadent food, wine and music extravaganza. Private dinners, celebrity chefs, culinary demonstrations, intimate musical entertainment, wine tastings, beer tastings, and a Sunday Supper all offer opportunities to meet fellow foodies.

Euphoria's Sunday Supper is one of its best events
Photo courtesy of Jivan Davé for Euphoria

Farm Fresh Festival – September
Enjoy live music, food and row after row of fun and funky furniture, antiques, jewelry and decor at this fall event at The Farm at Rabon Creek. Fountain Inn's lovely setting is home to farm animals and good old fashioned fresh air.

Indie Craft Parade – September
Handcrafted goods are celebrated with an inspiring weekend-long market that draws shoppers of all ages. This juried show offers everything from hand-printed stationery to canvas shoes.

Fall for Greenville – October
Over 40 restaurants showcase mouth-watering menu items during this signature downtown event. Concerts on five stages, wine and beer pairings, chef showcases and local hospitality competitions all add to the fun.

Holiday Events

Ice on Main – November through January
The green space at Courtyard by Marriott magically transforms into an urban ice rink below the city's Christmas tree. Skate rentals, steaming hot chocolate, and contraptions for novices all appear Thanksgiving weekend; skate into January.

Greenville Christmas Parade – December
Held the first Saturday after Thanksgiving, this fun family event is exactly what you'd expect: good old-fashioned fun on wheels. Santa? Of course!

Roper Mountain Holiday Lights – December
One of Greenville's simple pleasures, The Roper Mountain Science Center's annual Holiday Lights extravaganza offers a bevy of family fun: lighted trails, performances, and a 1.5 mile drive through large light displays coordinated to music.

Family Life

"It's divine to raise a family here," says Julie Karrer, mom of five kids ranging from 4 to 23. "There's no safer, happier location than Greenville. It's three hours to the ocean, an hour to the mountains. There's so much to do!" she says. "We literally have been surfing at Folly Beach one weekend and the next, camping at Pisgah Forest," says this active mom, whose adventurous husband Bert also takes the kids rock climbing.

The Karrers have another interesting idea when it comes to inspiration for family outings. "We change our memberships from year to year," Julie reveals. "We belong to the zoo one year, the fine art museum another year, so the kids are exposed to a lot of things, but don't burn out on any one thing."

Fun Fact: The **Children's Museum of the Upstate** is affiliated with the **Smithsonian Institution**, giving it access to Smithsonian collections, traveling exhibitions, scholarships and membership benefits.

Families love the area's many parks and playgrounds
Photo courtesy of GreenvilleRelocation.com

Area parks are another great focus for families. The city's massive **Cleveland Park** offers a huge recreational area for smaller kids, with loads of playground equipment and plenty of room to run. You'll find walking trails, tennis courts, volleyball pits, softball fields and basketball courts.

Cleveland Park is also home to **The Greenville Zoo**, a beloved family destination. The zoo offers zoo camp, Saturday safaris, "home schools" at the zoo, overnights, birthday parties, hands-on programs and a magical three-day Winter Vet Camp, where kids can use holiday time to learn about caring for animals.

Hot Tip: Check the zoo's website for upcoming events and to sign up for newsletters. If you follow the zoo on social media, you'll see news about upcoming births and **critter cams.**

From Cleveland Park, follow the Swamp Rabbit Trail to Falls Park. A dedicated outdoor stage area near the falls is home to summer's **Shakespeare in the Park** productions, a wonderful, free offering that can be enjoyed by the whole family. Downtown's own **splash park**, near the Hampton Inn hotel, is also fun. May's **Reedy River Duck Derby** is a must-do.

110

May's annual Reedy River Duck Derby at the Falls
Photo courtesy of D.J. Henson

Yet another resource for families is the **South Carolina Children's Theater** which hosts events like Kids Night Out, Princess Parties and holiday get-togethers. The **Children's Museum of the Upstate** offers field trips, camps, storytelling, contests and more; its website has event, newsletter and membership options.

On the same downtown campus, you'll find the **Greenville County Museum of Art**; the **Upcountry History Museum**, which brings the city to life in new ways; and the **Greenville Library** system's Hughes main facility. Eleven library branches and a bookmobile serve the entire area. You'll find sections for kids, teens and events on the library website.

A few times a year, **"Moonlight Movies"** are shown downtown, a fun evening out for the family. Your family can have the time of its life looking for **Mice on Main.** This innovative scavenger hunt, inspiration for a popular children's book available locally, encourages kids to seek out bronze mice which hide in plain sight on Main Street.

111

When it's warm out, the **Greenville County Rec Departments' outdoor water parks** are a must. Located in Mauldin, Simpsonville and Fountain Inn, these fun-filled destinations offer all sorts of temptations: water slides, a lazy river, sun decks, Flow-Rider®, body slides, a tube slide, a kiddie slide...you get the picture.

City and county parks are abundant, and offer year-round respite from being indoors. Greenville Rec also offers kids a total of eight different day camps, winter and spring break camps and after-school programs. Sign up for newsletters which can be tailored to your family's recreational interests.

Another favorite pastime of spring and summer is a night at **Fluor Field**. Cheer on **The Greenville Drive** baseball team (farm team for the Boston Red Sox) from the comfort of the stands, or your own blanket on the grassy hill behind third base. Friday nights are exciting: each and every one concludes with a fireworks show. And if your family loves sports, the **Greenville Swamp Rabbits** hockey team offers up rock-'em sock-'em entertainment on ice, also for very affordable ticket prices.

Downtown's **Kroc Center**, a state-of-the-art recreational and arts facility managed by the Salvation Army, created its welcoming **Teen Night**, when area teens get together for a meal and devotion topics chosen by the kids themselves. From a biblical standpoint, they discuss age-relevant issues they're struggling with, then head to the game room or gym. Churches all across town also offer **youth programs, church league basketball, life centers** for socializing, and other safe events.

Roper Mountain Science Center hosts all sorts of themed festivals—always with interactive components—as well as its Living History Farm, the Hall of Natural Science, more than 90 summer camps and a popular planetarium.

For even more ideas, follow **Kidding Around Greenville** on Facebook. It seems to have a wealth of ideas and information, plus offers email options.

112

Spiritual Life

Greenville is largely Christian. And it's Southern. Which means it's brimming with kind, compassionate and caring people. There are several other religions represented here but Christian churches dominate the landscape: the highest point in any community, in fact, typically holds a Baptist church with stellar views.

Google shows nearly 50 Presbyterian churches listed in the greater area, and about the same number of Methodist churches. There are a whopping 125 or so Baptist churches—one for every neighborhood—and several AME church homes. Catholics also have several choices.

Needless to say, the spiritual life is important in Greenville, so much so that longtime local church-goers reference God as naturally as they do their boss at work…but if faith isn't a big part of *your* life, and reading this even makes you nervous you'll fit in, *relax*. You're not likely to be pressured in any way…just treated with great kindness.

Pretty Place Chapel at YMCA Camp Greenville
Photo courtesy of D.J. Henson

113

Your brand of spirituality is a personal choice and locals treat it as such. Fair warning, though: should you be out in public on a Sunday from about 11:20 'til 1:00, you *may* feel a little out of place if casually dressed, when church-going families in their Sunday clothes start piling into area restaurants and stores.

If the idea of joining people of faith who share your beliefs *is* important to you—or is an appealing thought to pursue—you won't have any trouble finding a spiritual community of your own in Greenville. "Each church has a different personality; you'll find one to fit yours," says friendly longtime pastor Mike Cruice (who now gives relocation tours with Make Greenville Yours).

Greater Greenville has several large churches with **ministries for special groups and all ages:** singles, single parents, college students, seniors, teens, women, men.

The area's **largest places of worship**—enormous churches with huge campuses, multiple services and brimming event calendars—include First Baptist Greenville; Redemption World Outreach Church (Greenville); Taylors First Baptist Church (Taylors); Rock Springs Baptist (Easley); Brookwood (Simpsonville); and New Spring (Anderson).

A **variety of worship styles** are readily available here, from traditional to contemporary to modern. You'll find settings where coat and tie predominate, while elsewhere, you'd be comfortable with jeans and a flannel shirt. Televised services each Sunday morning are another option (and great to keep in mind on the rare inclement weather day).

Hot Tip: If you love Billy Graham, visit his library in nearby Charlotte. You might also enjoy televised or live services of the Spartanburg Baptist Church, where the pastor is a longtime friend of the Graham family.

"Some churches avoid the label of denomination," explains Cruice, of the term **'bible church.'** They don't want a label like Baptist or Presbyterian to be the thing that keeps somebody from coming to the church. What drives them is the bible, so they identify more with being a bible church."

114

Youth group's fun fall retreat at Look UP Lodge
Photo courtesy of First Presbyterian Church Greenville

Variety of Doctrines

Unitarians, Mormons and a host of other religious communities with a cultural affiliation all have a home in the Upstate. These include:

Vedic Center of Greenville (Hindu)
Hindu Society of Greater Spartanburg
Bethel Israel Synagogue (Jewish)
Temple of Israel (Jewish)
Islamic Society of Greenville (Muslim)
Carolina Buddhist Vihara
St. George Greek Orthodox Church
St. Mary's Coptic Orthodox Church (Egyptian)
– Provided by Greenville Economic Development

Fun Fact: While its history is no longer relative to its curriculum, Furman was founded as a Southern Baptist school, so has a Baptist heritage. The university is now secular, having broken from the Southern Baptist Convention about fifteen years ago. **North Greenville University** maintains its Southern Baptist roots.

Special Events

Renowned **Bob Jones University** is a Christian liberal arts university, its large campus within city limits. Bob Jones University's **Living Gallery** programs are a must-see undertaking of artists, technicians, actors, singers and musicians. They only happen rarely, but when they do, you want to be there. A talented team re-creates a Master painting depicting the life of Christ, in larger-than-life fashion, using sets, real actors, costumes, makeup, lighting and live music. The end result is difficult to capture with words but impossible to forget.

Social Life

Making friends is easy in Greenville, because everyone here is so friendly. Getting involved in activities you love makes getting to know people even easier. Here's a handy list of some ways you can kick off your social life.

Alumni Clubs: Check Facebook or Google to see if your U has a club here.

Church Events: Online calendars are available for many, including downtown's Christ Church, Brushy Creek Baptist, Brookwood Church in Simpsonville, Grace Church (7 locations), Greenville Unitarian Universalist Fellowship and Rock Springs Baptist in Easley.

Civic Clubs: Rotary International, Junior League, Business and Professional Women, The Elks Lodge…these groups all provide great networking opportunities, and one is likely a good fit for you. Rotary is particularly active in Greenville, with several chapters and a vibrant Rotary Youth Exchange program.

Classes: Furman's Osher Lifelong Learning Institute (OLLI) affords you friends and skills at the same time. Acorss the city, you'll also find classes for cooking, tennis, Spanish and woodworking. Or investigate the dance scene: shagging, swing and ballroom are all here.

Country Clubs: The upstate has several country clubs, and at all price points. Many allow social or sports memberships, and don't require property purchase. If you need a sponsor, speak with a golf or tennis pro about how to meet members.

116

Dining Clubs: Supper clubs are taking off in a big way in Greenville. Read more in the Food section of this book.

Attend free concerts at NOMA Square to meet people
Photo courtesy of D.J. Henson

Meetups: From board games to beer drinking to hiking there's an associated Greenville meetup group. Check out Meetup.com to find one or more that speak to you. You'll be amazed by the variety.

Newcomers Club: The Greenville Newcomers Club has a full slate of social activities on its calendar, and is a fun way to meet new folks while also learning more about the city.

Professional Organizations and Clubs: You'll be surprised how progressive our local Chamber of Commerce is: its expansive NEXT program fosters start-ups and tech businesses. Leadership classes, and all kinds of development and networking opportunities are also afforded to members.

Special Interest Clubs and Groups: From philanthropy to animal rescue, there's no shortage of special focus clubs to consider joining. Google Greenville + [your passion] and see what you find.

Sports Clubs: Like food, sports is a quick way to make friends. Check out places like the Kroc Tennis Center, The Sports Club or area golf clubs to meet compadres.

117

Volunteering: Clement's Kindness, The Julie Valentine Center, The Greenville Literacy Association, Project Host, Hands on Greenville or an arts organization like The Warehouse Theater are just a few of the deserving entities that would love to have your help.

Young Professionals Groups: Several area organizations have subsidiary groups which cater to young professionals 20-40, a way of fostering new support. Among the best are Greenville Symphony Orchestra's Downtown Symphony Club; Greenville County Museum of Art's Young Collectors; and the Greenville Chamber of Commerce's Pulse Young Professionals.

Sports

Greenville loves spectator sports as much as most cities, but probably edges out more than a few when it comes to *playing* sports. Our fantastic park systems and four mild seasons all combine to make the Upstate a paradise for golf, tennis, cycling, team sports and running.

Participatory Sports for Adults

Greenville Rec offers adults a winning number of sports through its partnerships with local clubs. These include badminton, bubble soccer, basketball, flag football, ice hockey, indoor soccer, inline hockey, kickball, lacrosse, soccer, softball, table tennis, tennis and volleyball. Area churches also organize basketball and softball leagues.

Fun Fact: Over 10,000 people participate in sports organized by Greenville Rec each year.

You'll have no trouble at all finding a **tennis** match, team or club, and both South Carolina and Greenville are extremely active in USTA. Tennis centers not associated with a neighborhood include The Kroc Center (Greenville); The Sports Club (Greenville, Simpsonville and Five Forks); Riverside and Tryon Park (both in Greer); and The Greenville Tennis Club (in Five Forks). Freedom Tennis League offers flex schedules. **Pickleball** and **racquetball** are easy to find.

118

Kroc Center's winning 'Love Means Nothing' tennis team
Photo courtesy of The Kroc Center

Golf courses include The Preserve at Verdae Golf Club, Paris Mountain Country Club and several rural options (often more affordable), including Rolling Greens, Southern Oaks, Pickens County Country Club and Saluda Valley. The appealing Furman University course is open to the public, while affordable Bonnie Brae lies to the south, near SCTAC. **Par Three** courses include Carolina Golf and Tennis Club and Crosswinds Golf Course (near downtown). Fountain Inn's Fox Run Country Club and Carolina Springs Country Club are two more options for golf play.

SEE ALSO: Where to Live: **Golf Communities**

If you love **swimming**, Greenville Rec's **Westside Aquatic Complex**, on west Blue Ridge Drive, offers the state's only enclosed public 50-meter pool. You'll also find indoor pools at The Caine Halter YMCA, The Life Center and downtown's Kroc Center (Caine-Halter also has an outdoor pool).

Sports for the Kids

Through the county's amazing **Greenville Rec** department, kids can compete in organized baseball and softball, basketball, BMX, competitive swimming, flag football, football, ice hockey, ice skating, inline hockey, lacrosse, soccer and tennis.

119

Greenville County **middle schools and high schools** offer all the sports you'd expect, plus a few you might not, including boys and girls **cross country, lacrosse, swimming** and **competitive cheer**.

Greenville HS students build camaraderie through sports
Photo courtesy of Stacey Krall

The **Greenville Gymnastics Training Center** has programs for all skill levels and has been part of the community for over 20 years. The **Wenwood Soccer Complex** in **Mauldin** is home of the Carolina Elite Soccer Academy. You'll find six soccer fields at this busy 49-acre park, along with a picnic shelter and playground.

Across the street, Mauldin's **Conestee Park**, original home of the former Greenville Braves AA baseball team, is now a fully renovated baseball stadium with four additional diamonds with batting cages and bullpens. Home of Greenville Little League, this popular park has hosted competitive Senior League (MSBL) and college baseball events.

Fun Fact: Outfields at two Conestee Park baseball diamonds mimic Camden Yards and Nationals Park.

Corey Burns Park in **Taylors**, with its five baseball fields, was home to the inspirational **Northwood Little League Team**, which made it to the 2015 Little League World Series.

120

Spectator Sports

Everybody loves going to **Greenville Drive** baseball games. Fluor Field is a great ballpark and it's great fun to cheer for players working their way toward the Red Sox organization.

Fluor Field has a special hill just for families
Photo courtesy of GreenvilleRelocation.com

Hot Tip: Baseball fans are blown away by the Shoeless Joe Jackson Museum in downtown Greenville, located right behind Fluor Field. It's truly fantastic.

The **Greenville Swamp Rabbits** ECHL team brings out fans in droves during season. Throw on a jacket, head to the Bon Secours Arena downtown and cheer for the guys whose slogan is 'Fear the Ears.'

Furman University plays basketball in Timmons Arena, and the men's and women's tennis teams are both fantastic to watch. As mentioned in the Local Culture chapter, football is a very, very big deal here. Jump right into the local scene with the purchase of tickets to see the Furman Paladins, **Clemson Tigers** or **Carolina Gamecocks** football teams.

Hot Tips: The Charlotte Panthers train at Spartanburg's Wofford College during the NFL pre-season, and the public can watch. NFL team schedules may also reveal a team from your previous hometown coming to the region.

121

If the roar of an engine makes your heart race, you'll love being near the heart of **NASCAR** (many teams are based in nearby Charlotte and its famous Motor Speedway). But it's also fun to run over to Easley for a night of rip-roaring fun at the **Greenville Pickens Speedway.** Several NASCAR teams actually use the facility to practice for short-track races.

May's annual **BMW Charity Pro-Am golf tournament** brings many popular PGA stars to Greenville's most beautiful golf courses (and there are also playing opportunities for the public).

Fun Fact: Because tickets to The Masters were originally sold regionally, more than a few Greenville families have at least a pair of tickets each year; the rest of the world relies on winning the Augusta National lottery (odds are better than for Powerball, but tough, nonetheless).

Wellness

Greenville's beautiful setting lends itself to an active, outdoor lifestyle. The Swamp Rabbit Trail stays busy, as do local parks, sports facilities and gyms. But you have nearly unlimited options for indoor workouts as well, including with trainers and counselors. Recognizable brands like **Planet Fitness, Crossfit** and **Gold's Gym** all have a healthy presence in the Upstate.

The massive Caine-Halter **YMCA** complex near downtown has outdoor and indoor pools, dry sauna, steam room, a walking track, cycling, cardio and strength equipment, yoga classes, a cycling studio and a place to leave your kids while you work out. There are other popular YMCA facilities at Verdae and in Simpsonville, Taylors and Travelers Rest.

GHS's architecturally beautiful **Life Center,** near downtown, is another magnet for people whose routine includes a workout. It holds indoor and outdoor tracks, a 25-meter indoor pool, dry sauna and children's area, while offering aerobics, cycling, Pilates, yoga, massage, nutrition counseling, and medically based programs.

Greenville Health System's Life Center
Photo courtesy of GHS

Be aware that several of the **larger churches** in the area also have extremely active **wellness facilities** with fitness programs, including league basketball. Some, like Redemption World Outreach's **Imagine Center** (on Haywood Road) are open to the public.

PureBarre has a Greenville location (Augusta Road) while independent studios offering **yoga**, **hot yoga** and **Pilates** are popular and easy to find in the area. You'll even find eastern **qijong** yoga and workshops, as well as **tai chi**. You can enjoy regular discounts from massage practices and spas by keeping an eye on LivingSocial and Groupon while discounted **massage** prices are offered year-round to those who make a treatment commitment at **Massage Envy** locations.

Several places offer **kickboxing**, including **9Round**'s multiple locations and **CKO**, but you'll also find classes and clubs online. If you're interested in **cycling for fitness**, Greenville is the perfect place to plug in, at any level. Talk to the friendly folks in an outfitter or bike shop, join a MeetUp group, or look for group ride opportunities, which are widely advertised on posters and social media.

For the 60+ Set

Whatever your lifestyle (or that of the folks 60+ in your life), you'll appreciate a few Greenville qualities in particular. The city's pace is not frantic, drivers are courteous, people are kind, children are well-mannered and elders are respected. Educational opportunities are also abundant. How's that sound?

Greenville has a very active older population. Stop by the Kroc Tennis Center and you'll be amazed how many **55-and-over tennis teams** play there and in other tennis clubs across the city. The area's **golf courses** stay busy, and winter months see many a day when they're playable.

*Hot Tip: Check out the semi-private **Saluda Valley Country Club** in Williamston (SW of town) which offers a relatively flat (but still pretty) and very affordable course with wide fairways. Walking is allowed.*

Several area churches have programs and social groups designed specifically for seniors. Greenville County's many libraries also host guest speakers and special programs, while offering music, movies, large-print books and a nice place to hang out. Osher Lifelong Learning Institute (OLLI) courses provide mental stimulation, socialization and recreational opportunities.

Here's some really great news: The state of South Carolina's **Plan 60 option** allows any legal resident aged 60 or older, who is not employed full-time, to attend most continuing education or curriculum classes on a space available basis **without payment.** The class must have reached its minimum enrollment and have space available. Then you're in!

Programs are created especially for seniors by Greenville Rec, at six different **community centers**. The County also hosts a **Senior Sports Classic**, the occasional organized walk, and a **retreat** designed especially for the "more experienced" set.

Music from previous eras can be enjoyed in **The Poinsett Hotel lobby**, or at **The Phoenix Inn** on Pleasantburg. Furman University, The Greenville Little Theater, The SC Governor's School and even Pecknel Music Company offer free or affordable concerts. A full list of **free concerts which happen downtown** on

Thursdays, Fridays and Saturdays is listed in the Arts & Entertainment chapter. (Yes, you can bring your own chair).

Greenville's non-profit **Senior Action Center** provides transportation, meals, home care management and fitness programs, but also gives seniors social and volunteer opportunities, optional travel excursions and continuing education.

The **Appalachian Area Agency on Aging (AAAOA)** out of the Lieutenant Governor's office (located next to Mackey Mortuary off Century Drive) is the ombudsman and resource center for many senior issues, such as Medicare, nursing homes, assisted-living and more.

SEE ALSO: Where to Live: **Retirement Communities**

Hiking, Cycling and Adventure

Greenville's location in the Blue Ridge foothills makes it a recreational paradise nearly year-round. Within an hour or less, you can be hiking alongside a beautiful mountain creek, photographing a waterfall, swimming with your dog in a pristine lake, cycling past vineyards, or watching sunset from a mountaintop. In less than two hours, you can be enjoying parks, trails, vistas and villages in the mountains of western North Carolina and up on the Blue Ridge Parkway, but also in beautiful north Georgia. That's part of the magic.

Hot Tip: Furman University has 13 miles of paved woodland trails for hiking; one trail circles its beautiful lake.

Hiking

"I have folks come in here all the time who are new to the area and wanting to get into hiking," says lifelong resident Jay Ferguson, Assistant Manager at Half Moon Outfitters. Although you just need hiking shoes and a water bottle, Half Moon also sells clothing , all sorts of gear, kayaks, tents, maps and books. Ferguson, who estimates being familiar with 90% of Upstate trails, tells inquiring customers "what they're about to get into," referring to levels of difficulty, and tips he happily shares (like always letting someone know where you're going and when you'll return).

125

Jones Gap, in northern Greenville County, has creekside trails
Photo courtesy of D.J. Henson

Ready to take your **first local hike**? "Right out of Greenville, I always recommend **Paris Mountain**," he says. "It's 15 minutes from here, and it's open seven days a week. Try to get out during the week, it's not quite as crowded with the mountain bikes and hikers that come on weekends." Paris Mountain does close to biking on Saturdays. "There are also a few hike-only trails," says Ferguson.

Hot Tip: Connect with the friendly Greenville Natural History Association to make friends who go on organized hikes.

According to Ferguson, a must-do hike is **Table Rock State Park**, in the north part of the county. "There are 360 degree views up there. Hiking to the top," he says, "is not easy—round trip is five hours—but it's definitely doable, and it's beautiful." Needless to say, any fall hike is spectacular, as the Blue Ridge Mountains explode into reds, oranges and yellows. The highest point in South Carolina—Sassafras Mountain—offers unparalleled views.

126

Fun Fact: **Audubon** designated the **Jocassee Gorges** one of the world's internationally **Important Bird Areas**, its peregrine falcons and bald eagles continually exciting to watch or photograph. It joins Caesars Head State Park, Table Rock State Park, Sumter National Forest and Hogback Mountain on this list.

Cycling

There's a palpable passion for cycling here, and it's actually bringing in tourism and new residents, thanks in large part to the high-profile advocacy of champion cyclist and local resident George Hincapie. About 2,000 people attended Hincapie's 2015 Gran Fondo, hailed by Men's Journal as one of the best in the country. Hincapie's **Hotel Domestique** and the rolling hills surrounding it are big draws to road cyclists throughout the year.

Cycling is a way of life for many Greenville residents. You'll meet a combination of competitive road racers, recreational road cyclists, mountain bikers, and recreational pedalers who ply the **Swamp Rabbit Trail** and other routes they enjoy. The Swamp Rabbit traverses Cleveland Park and Falls Park, runs north past Furman, then through downtown Travelers Rest.

The Swamp Rabbit Trail stretches toward North Carolina
Photo courtesy of D.J. Henson

127

Leisure road cyclists often ride up to the bakery in Saluda, NC. "You can ride from North Greenville University," says Jay Ferguson, "and round-trip, it's like 35 miles. You're mainly climbing on the way up, and then descending through the watershed on the way back." **Mountain Bikers** are a surprisingly mixed group by age, according to Ferguson, and enjoy their sport 12 months a year. Ferguson's a fan of Greenville Rec's **Pleasant Ridge** (on Highway 11) and **Paris Mountain**, both of which have trails.

Local outfitters and bike shops have expert outdoorsmen on staff, and carry books and maps on regional outdoors topics. Posters and flyers promote upcoming events, while brochures detail area guides. In addition to **Half Moon Outfitters**, you'll find **Appalachian Outfitters**, **Mast General**, **Trek Bicycle Store**, **Carolina Triathlon**, **TTR Bikes** and **Sunrift** (in T.R.). On a larger scale, you'll find **REI**, **Cabela's** and several big-box stores, including **Academy Sports**, along Woodruff Road.

Other Adventures

Ziplining, trail running, paddling, fishing, SUP and rock climbing round out the other most popular sports in the area.

Hot Tip: Check out The Mountain Goat nonprofit indoor climbing gym, raising money to take underprivileged kids on adventures.

Getting on the Water

You may not realize that Greenville is a short drive from some of the most beautiful lakes, rivers and waterfalls in the world—literally.

The Lakes

Nearby **Lake Jocassee** is, in a word, breathtaking. Nearly 100% protected from development along its shoreline, this pristine 7,500 acre haven—with its panoramic Blue Ridge Mountain views—makes a perfect destination for all sorts of watersports (including scuba diving), picnics and family fun. Lake Jocassee is encompassed by the **Jocassee Gorges** area, named by **National Geographic** in 2012 as one of '**50 of the World's Last Great Places.**'

Lake Jocassee is unparalleled for views
Photo courtesy of D.J. Henson

Hot Tip: Devils Fork State Park affords the only public access to Lake Jocassee, and can also accommodate overnight guests in its fully-furnished villas or within two campgrounds located near the lake.

Lake Keowee, just below Jocassee in the same chain of lakes near the Georgia border, offers similarly amazing mountain views and clear water. It's home to several luxury neighborhoods but offers spectacular recreational opportunities to non-resident paddlers and boaters who trailer or rent.

Lake Hartwell, at the bottom of the chain, wraps around the Clemson campus. The water here is not as clear, but Hartwell is much more accessible for recreational purposes.

Closer to Greenville's southwest side, **Lake Saluda** is fed by the **Saluda River** and has residential neighborhoods around it. Just south of Tigerville, in northern Greenville County, **Lake (John A.) Robinson** offers a smaller but still beautiful setting. Several residential neighborhoods ring this lake and you'll find a lovely park on its south side. Spring means the waiting is over for water enthusiasts.

Watersports

"Paddle sports is really big here," says Half Moon Bay Outfitter's Jay Ferguson. "Many people will get a **paddleboard** or a **kayak** and leave it at the lake, if they can." Toward Spartanburg," he says, "there are a couple of wider rivers that offer **calmer paddling**, like the **Tyger**, or the **French Broad** from Rosman through Asheville. You can reserve a campsite along the river," says Ferguson. "There are no crazy rapids, maybe a Class 1 at the most." Whitewater kayaking is big with many locals, though, who find lots of nearby opportunities.

SUP (stand-up paddleboarding) is also big here. When you're standing five to six feet off the water at Jocassee, you can see 15 to 20 feet down. "A lot of folks are doing SUP yoga," says Ferguson. "I know a couple of folks that will take groups out to Jocassee or Keowee to do SUP yoga on the weekends." During the summer, you won't need a wetsuit, but in the winter, it's recommended.

Some of the best **trout fishing** in the state can be enjoyed at **Devils Fork State Park**, on beautiful Lake Jocassee.

Hot Tip: Lake Cunningham Recreation Facility Pier offers **handicap-accessible** *fishing, but the DNR website says it has a goal of enhancing access in several facilities.*

Swimming can be enjoyed at Paris Mountain and Table Rock, while nearby **waterfalls** are so abundant, you can reach many from here with a short drive. There are falls you hike to easily, others which take a commitment to reach by foot, falls you can actually walk behind, falls to slide down, and one you can even drive beneath. Dupont Forest is not only close but is a favorite: its three falls are all within easy hiking distance.

It's a Dog's Life

Between our great weather and the city's abundance of paths, parks and green spaces, you and your four-footed companions are sure to make a great life here. You'll find dog spas, camps, mobile grooming, locally made organic treats, all the typical big-box stores, and several appealing small shops which are dedicated to dog-centric lifestyles.

Generally, **restaurants** will allow dogs on their patios. And you can have your dog in the city's beautiful **downtown** as long as it's on a leash, under control and not aggressive. You'll also find **water bowls** plentiful; lots of business owners are dog lovers or owners.

Greenville is paradise for dog lovers
Photo courtesy of GreenvilleRelocation.com

What to Do Together

Your list of places to explore should start with the welcoming dog park at **Conestee Park in Mauldin.** Easy to reach just off I-85, Conestee offers pooches fenced play areas delineated by dog size; benches for companions; watering stations; special dog play features; a large expanse of grass for running together and places to splash around. A huge network of trails is adjacent.

Downtown's **Cleveland Park** is Dog Central, where you'll meet dog-loving residents along the Swamp Rabbit Trail. Also popular is the beautiful **Furman University campus,** its **picturesque lake** ringed by a dog-friendly trail.

Taylors has two county parks with facilities just for you: the **Pelham Mill Dog Park** and the **Pavilion Recreation Complex Dog Park.** Just north of downtown, beautiful **Paris Mountain State Park** offers even more opportunities for communing with nature.

131

For a special day of hiking, splashing and swimming in Carolina's beautiful mountain rivers, head to stunning **Jones Gap**. "Our dogs love to wade in the streams there," reveals The Humane Society's Bonnie Wallin, who also takes her pets to **Caesars Head**, a nearby state park offering a dozen marked trails. Don't miss this park's stunning overlook of Table Rock in the distance, and **Table Rock State Park** also welcomes leashed dogs on its trails.

The Humane Society is adjacent to the downtown airport
Photo courtesy of GreenvilleRelocation.com

Don't miss the **Mutt Strut** in late August; it's the largest dog-friendly race in South Carolina and has toys, games, a marketplace and a band. "We had 1,000 dogs last year," says Bonnie Wallin, with a smile. **Bark in the Park** and the **Tails & Trails 5K** are two more events for your calendar.

Greenville Humane Society

This amazing no-kill shelter, clinic and adoption center is one of the gemstones in the city's crown. It offers low-cost vaccinations and spay/neuter services, and can also connect you with a reputable veterinarian. If you'd like to get further involved, you can volunteer to work on site, or as a pet therapy facilitator for local senior centers.

132

Award-Winning Care

Upstate Veterinary Specialists, a local full-service animal hospital has been named "Animal Specialty Hospital of the Year in the U.S. and Canada," by the American Animal Hospital Association (AAHA). It provides advanced medical, surgical, oncological, dental and eye care for pets. A regular veterinarian must refer your pet to this facility, which is located near the downtown airport. Many of the clinic's minimally invasive procedures happen in comfortable suites.

Adjacent to UVS is the Animal Emergency Clinic, which handles **nighttime emergencies**, 6 p.m. to 8 a.m.

Conestee Nature Park's dedicated dog park
Photo courtesy of GreenvilleRelocation.com

Dog Laws You Need to Know

The city of Greenville has its own animal control laws, as do Mauldin, Simpsonville, Greer and Travelers Rest. Other areas are under county jurisdiction. Check the laws for your area, but leash laws and nuisance ordinances are fairly universal. State law requires vaccinations and a rabies tag. Even though Greenville has a temperate climate, no dog is equipped for outside weather 12 months a year. If authorities find an animal in an enclosed car in summer, they will get it out and the owner will be ticketed.

133

Great Day Trips

Whether you prefer hiking to waterfalls, exploring an appealing mountain village or festival, tubing down a mountain river, or feeding goats on the roof (yes, that is possible!), you need only drive a short distance from Greenville to do it.

Here's a list of some favorite day trips, sans details, but divided by topic, making it easier for you to choose your next adventure.

Amazing Mother Nature

Bald Rock and Caesars Head, SC

Chimney Rock - Lake Lure, NC

Cullasaja River Gorge and Falls - Highlands, NC

Dupont State Forest - Cedar Mountain, NC

Jones Gap State Park - Marietta, SC

Lake Jocassee & Devils Fork State Park - Oconee County, SC

Mount Mitchell - near Black Mountain, NC

Sassafras Mountain - near Rocky Bottom, SC

South Carolina Botanical Garden - Clemson, SC

Table Rock State Park - Highway 11

Historic Places

Abbeville, SC

Edgefield, SC

Cherokee, NC

Campbell's Covered Bridge - SC

Carl Sandburg Estate - Flat Rock, NC

Cowpens National Battlefield - SC

Hagood Mill - Pickens, SC

Foodie Treks

Grits and Groceries - Belton, SC

James Beard restaurants - Asheville, NC

Skytop Orchard - Flat Rock, NC

WNC Cheese Trail - Asheville, NC

Cool Villages & Towns

Black Mountain, NC

Brevard, NC

Cashiers, NC

Clayton, GA

Dahlonega, GA

Dillard, GA

Flat Rock, NC

Helen, GA

Hendersonville, NC

Highlands, NC

Lake Lure, NC

Landrum, SC

Saluda, NC

Tryon, NC

Oddities, Wonders & Iconic Landmarks

Billy Graham Library - Charlotte, NC

Biltmore Estate - Asheville, NC

Blue Ridge Parkway - NC and VA

Goats on the Roof - Clayton, GA

'Pretty Place' Chapel - Marietta, GA

Stumphouse Mountain Tunnel - Walhalla, SC

Tryon Equestrian Center - Mill Spring, NC

Get inspired for your own day trips!
Follow **BlueRidgeWeekends**
online and on social.

134

CHAPTER 5:
HANDY REFERENCE SECTION

Licenses, Registrations & Taxes

The complex called **County Square** is where you'll conduct much of your government business, including property and probate, vehicle registrations, licenses and more. There's loads of parking here, and the complex, at Church and University Ridge, is clearly marked, so you know which entrance to use.

Hot Tip: The City's free trolley comes to this parking lot during Greenville Drive ballgames, so it's a great place to park and ride. It's also a short stroll from here to Falls Park and the historic West End.

Driver's License:
DMV Office (multiple locations, including across from County Square)

The law says you have 90 days to get a South Carolina driver's license. BEWARE you need a fair amount of documentation to get a driver's license—likely more than you're used to providing—but the good news is that the DMV can also forward your information to the South Carolina election commission so that you're simultaneously registered to vote.

All applicants for driver's licenses must provide ALL of the following:
1. Proof of S.C. Residency
2. Proof of U.S. Citizenship (birth certificate, passport)
3. Proof of Social Security Number
4. Automobile liability insurance information

Vehicle Registration & Tax:
County Square on University Ridge

You're required to register your car in the county, and it will be taxed each year, based on value. (Example: a four-year-old mid-range SUV was $400-$500 in 2015). Go to the Auditor's Office, Suite 800 at County Square on University

136

Ridge Road. Show them your current registration and they'll give you a tax bill, which you must take to Suite 700 to pay. Then you'll need to take your receipt across the street to the DMV to obtain a license plate, proof of registration (to be kept in your car) and sticker for your tag.

Voter Registration:
County Square on University Ridge

Applications must be received by the voter registration office (or be postmarked) PRIOR to the 30th day before an election. You'll need a valid S.C. driver's license or DMV ID, which means you must first update your address with the DMV. You can register online, by mail or in person. For the mail option, you'll need to download the application from scVOTES.org, or pick it up at the County Square offices, then mail it along with a photocopy of your ID. Acceptable IDs for registering to vote include a current valid photo ID; or a paycheck, government document, bank statement or utility bill showing your name and address in the county.

Property Tax

South Carolina state law taxes all owner-occupied homes at a rate of 4% and other properties—second homes, rental homes, commercial properties—at a rate of 6%. Cities can levy additional taxes. To understand more about this tax, go to pages 76 and 77 of this book.

State Income Tax

The South Carolina Department of Revenue website says:

Your federal taxable income is the starting point in determining your state income tax liability. Individual income tax rates range from 0% to a top rate of 7% on taxable income. Tax brackets are adjusted annually for inflation.

2015 South Carolina Income Tax Table	
Tax Bracket	Marginal Tax Rate
$0+	0.00%
$2,880+	3.00%
$5,760+	4.00%
$8,640+	5.00%
$11,520+	6.00%
$14,400+	7.00%

Check with your tax preparation professional; rates can change.

137

Population & Demographics

Populations

The Greenville-Anderson-Mauldin Metropolitan Statistical Area (MSA), consists of Greenville, Anderson, Pickens and Laurens Counties.

City of Greenville: 62,252   **Greenville MSA:** 862,463
Greenville County: 482,752   **South Carolina:** 4,774,839

Demographics - Greenville County

Age		
Under 10	13.2%	
10 to 19	12.9%	
20 to 34	20.4%	
35 to 54	27%	
55 to 64	12.3%	
65 and older	14.3%	
Median Age	37.7% (2013)	
59.7% of population is age 20-64		
Race		
White	371,425	76.9%
Black or African American	89,281	18.5%
Hispanic or Latino	42,309	8.7%
Asian	10,761	2.2%
Two or More Races	8,399	1.7%
Amer. Indian / Alaskan	2,546	0.5%
Education		
HS Graduate or Higher	86.4% of people 25+	
Bachelor's Degree or Higher	31.2% of people 25+	
Earnings		
Median Household Income	$49,476 (2013)	
Per Capita Income	$32,913 (2014)	
Gender		
Male	234,668	48.6%
Female	248,084	51.4%

South Carolina Facts to Know

Population: 4.9 million
Date of Statehood: 1788
State Animal: White-tailed deer
State Bird: Carolina wren
State Capital: Columbia

Largest Cities, in order: Columbia, Charleston, North Charleston, Greenville, Rock Hill, Mount Pleasant, Spartanburg, Hilton Head, Florence, Goose Creek.

Fun Facts: The **state flag** depicts the **sabal palm**, the state tree. Fibrous Sabal palms successfully held off British cannonballs at Fort Moultrie (then called Fort Sullivan) during the Revolutionary War, when future namesake Colonel Moultrie scored a huge victory for The Patriots. (Fort Moultrie is near Charleston and can be visited by the public). Scholars agree that the flag's crescent represents a metal **crescent** found on Revolutionary uniforms, and not a moon, as is commonly thought.

State Dance: The Shag
This popular dance (especially with the over-50 crowd) is a version of swing, and is done to the state's official music, "**Beach Music**," a regional genre born of R&B, rock and pop influence in the 1950s. Beach Music and The Shag are responsible for wider acceptance of R&B by a white audience. Today, you'll still find dance nights and contests dedicated to both.

State Flower: Yellow jessamine (a.k.a. jasmine, a derivation)
State Fruit: Peach
State Nickname: The Palmetto State
State Tree: Sabal Palmetto
State Wildflower: Goldenrod

Big Moment in History: The first shots of the Civil War were fired at Fort Sumter (near Charleston) when Confederate forces decided to oust its occupying Union troops. South Carolina was the first state to secede from the U.S.

A Brief History of Greenville

1768 - Richard Pearis settles near the Reedy River
1795 - US Post Office opens
1815 - Vardry McBee builds grist mill on the river; buys 11,000 acres
1851 - Furman University moves here from North Carolina
1875 - First textile mill within city limits opens
1908 - Shoeless Joe Jackson shoots to national fame
1942 - Greenville Army Air Base opens
1947 - Bob Jones University moves here from Tennessee
1951 - Army Air Base is renamed Donaldson
1958 - Furman University moves to Poinsett Highway campus
1962 - Donaldson Air Force Base closes; GSP airport opens
1962 - Classes begin at Greenville Technical College
1974 - Heritage Green cultural campus is founded
1980 - Greenville considered "Textile Capital of the World"
1982 - Downtown's Hyatt opens; revitalization begins
1984 - Lockheed Martin maintenance & modification center opens
1987 - Michelin opens North American headquarters in Greer

1990 - Peace Center opens
1994 - BMW opens its first U.S. manufacturing plant, in Greer
1998 - 16,000 seat downtown arena opens
1999 - Co. Economic Development Corp. buys Swamp Rabbit rail bed
2000 - The Westin Poinsett opens, following massive renovation
2002 - Bridge over the Reedy River is razed, exposing falls
2003 - Falls Park, with Liberty Bridge, opens
2004 - CU-ICAR opens
2005 - Capital City Bombers (Red Sox farm team) move to Greenville
2006 - Fluor Field opens; Greenville Bombers become Greenville Drive
2008 - Donaldson renamed S.C. Tech and Aviation Center (SC-TAC)
2009 - NEXT Innovation Center opens
2010 - NY Rangers-affiliated hockey team moves here as Road Warriors
2010 - Clemson MBA program moves to downtown
2010 - Swamp Rabbit Trail opens
2012 - First class held at four-year USC School of Medicine
2013 - South Carolina's Inland Port opens in Greer
2014 - National accolades in travel, lifestyle start to appear regularly
2015 - Downtown redevelopment boom brings apartments, hotels
2015 - ECHL Road Warriors renamed Greenville Swamp Rabbits

Names You'll See & Who They Are

Anderson, Major Rudolph

This Greenville native was the only person killed by enemy fire during the Cuban Missile Crisis. You'll find a memorial in Cleveland Park; look for the airplane.

Cleveland, William Choice

In 1924, this former banker gifted 110 acres of land on the Reedy River and Richland Creek for Cleveland Park.

Daniel, Charles

Founded Daniel Construction in 1935, which built commercial, industrial and military installations around the world. The company was acquired by Fluor Corp in 1977, creating one of the largest engineering and construction companies in the world.

141

Hampton, Wade III
He's not from Greenville, but the 77th Governor of South Carolina has a local high school and an important road named after him. Hampton served as a Confederate general in the Civil War and also became a U.S. Senator.

Haas, Jay and Bill
Winning pro golfers from Greenville. Father Jay now plays the Champions Tour; son Bill competes in the PGA, and at the end of 2015 was ranked in the top 50.

Hipp family
The family patriarch established the Liberty Corporation (Liberty Life), which exploded financially by affordably insuring mill workers in the '20s. Branching into media, the Hipp family has long used its influence for education and environmental issues. Anna Kate Hipp was key to Falls Park's beginning.

Hughes family
Father "Red" was instrumental to the city's 1960s building boom. Sons Bob and Phil led the development of Riverplace and Main Street's TD bank building. Bob developed the environmentally-friendly mixed-use ONE Building and is active in many philanthropic endeavors. Phil has developed several innovative riverfront buildings and is an active supporter of local nonprofit endeavors, including the Hughes Library (the main branch of the county's library system).

Jackson, Jesse
Famous influencer Jesse Jackson was born in Greenville and lived here through high school graduation. He worked for Dr. Martin Luther King, Jr. and went on to national fame as a two-time presidential candidate and international activist.

Jackson, Shoeless Joe
America's most controversial baseball player hailed from Greenville, SC, where he is beloved to this day. Visit the bronze sculpture of him on south Main Street, or go deep, with a visit to the world-class Shoeless Joe Jackson Museum. You'll learn the story of this talented native son, and discover an astounding library of baseball tomes; authors come from all over the world to tap its resources.

Jones, Bob
Evangelist Bob Jones, Sr. founded the Greenville-based university which

142

bears this name. His son, Bob Jr., became the second president and Bob Jones III served as its third. The university is known for its conservative religious positions and renowned religious art collection.

Martin, Ben

By 2015, PGA player Ben Martin was ranked in the top 100, had his first PGA tourney win, and was making Clemson University proud. You can see this Greenville resident on TV, at local charity tournaments or simply around town.

McBee, Vardry

The true father of Greenville, wealthy McBee was the city's first entrepreneur. He built a tannery, a general store, a rock quarry and grist, corn, cotton, paper and woolen mills. He gifted parcels from his 11,000 acre holding—what is now downtown—for four church campuses. He was instrumental in the railroad's arrival. Remnants of one of McBee's mills still stand along the Reedy River.

McCain, Edwin

This popular singer-songwriter and talented musician was raised in Greenville and still makes his home here. His big hits 'I'll Be' and 'I Could Not Ask for More' made him famous, and he still performs occasionally, but also owns a recording studio. McCain co-founded the acclaimed Euphoria food, wine and music festival.

Mickel family

The late Buck Mickel negotiated the significant Fluor-Daniel merger. He was also instrumental to the opening of GSP airport. Buck's daughter Minor Mickel Shaw, a member of the SC Business Hall of Fame, chairs the GSP airport commission and serves as trustee and chairman of several endowments and foundations.

Peace family

This influential media family bought the Greenville News in 1919, before buying another newspaper and starting the city's first radio station. Their Multimedia Inc. company eventually went nationwide. The family's philanthropy resulted in downtown's Peace Center for the Performing Arts; they also contributed to the first rehabilitation hospital in the Upstate.

Pearis, Richard

Greenville's Paris Mountain uses a different spelling but was named for the

143

area's first white settler, an Indian trader. Pearis moved his wife and kids here after 1770 and set up a plantation along the Reedy. He allegedly had another child by a chief's daughter, and raids were staged at his plantation, despite his Presbyterian background.

Poinsett, Joel

The first Minister to Mexico under Andrew Jackson, Poinsett—an amateur but accomplished botanist—brought back the red Christmas flower which was then renamed for him. He served as a Secretary of War; started the Army Corps of Engineers; and ordered the haunting Trail of Tears evacuation before becoming the first president of the Smithsonian Institution. A bridge, highway, downtown hotel and private club also bear his name.

Rama family

This successful family of four brothers hailing from India are the brains behind JHM Hotels, which owns 40+ brand-name hotels, primarily in the Southeast. JHM bought downtown's landmark Hyatt Hotel in 2009, fully renovating it in 2013.

Robelot, Jane

Former CBS morning anchor and Greenville native; now lives here again.

Spinks family

Patriarch Stewart Spinks founded the company which owns the Spinx gas and convenience stores you'll see across the Upstate. Spinx sponsors events and organizations that improve children's lives, as well as golf and cycling events.

Timmons family

The patriarch of this real estate and insurance family purchased Canal Insurance in 1942, which grew to a nationwide company. The family profited from a development flurry in the '50s and '60s that saw 3,000-plus lots developed in the Wade Hampton area, then made Furman's namesake arena possible.

Townes, Dr. Charles H.

This 1964 Nobel prize winner had the idea that led to the invention of the laser. He also invented WWII radar bombing systems, was a lunar landing advisor, and helped discover the Milky Way's black hole.

144

White, Knox

Hailing from a family with a long history of public service, Mayor White is the longest-serving mayor in city history. A fervent, knowledgeable proponent of smart urban revitalization, White spearheaded removal of Camperdown Bridge, which made possible the realization of Falls Park. He led the efforts to bring baseball to downtown, and to reopen the Poinsett Hotel.

Wyche family

Longtime attorney and visionary Tommy Wyche helped attract the Hyatt to downtown, spurring the city's revitalization. He championed the Peace Center and envisioned the mixed-use River Place, along the Reedy. Tommy's greatest legacy is the Naturaland Trust, which preserved 40,000 acres of the Upstate, including Jocassee Gorges, Jones Gap State Park and Caesar's Head State Park. Wife Harriett was president of the Carolina Foothills Garden Club and a steadfast advocate for a public garden at the falls, which became Falls Park. Son Brad founded the influential organization Upstate Forever.

Born here or lived here: Peabo Bryson, Joanne Woodward, pro football player Andre Goodman, actress Jaimie Alexander, chef and TV host Tyler Florence, The Voice competitor Delvin Choice, weatherman Mike Seidel.

Local Media

Find these resources online, on social, on the radio, or on the newsstand. They'll really help you assimilate your new Greenville life, and keep abreast of what's happening, as well as who's who.

At Home – seasonal lifestyle magazine
Business Black Box – quarterly business magazine
Edible Upcountry magazine – quarterly food magazine
Fete Greenville TV – weekly YouTube calendar videos
Fete Greenville Magazine – monthly digital magazine
Greenville Business Magazine – monthly
Greenville Journal – weekly newspaper
GSA Business – biweekly magazine with Upstate focus
South Carolina ETV – (Public Television)

Talk Magazine – monthly lifestyles magazine
The Greenville News – daily newspaper
The Scout Guide / Greenville – digital and print magazine
TOWN Magazine – monthly lifestyles magazine
Upstate Business Journal – weekly newspaper
USA TODAY 10Best (digital) – Greenville lists and articles
WSPA (CBS) Spartanburg – network television
WYFF (NBC) Greenville – network television
WLOS (ABC) Asheville – network television
WHNS (FOX) Greenville – network television
ETV (PBS) Columbia – public television
UNC-TV (PBS) Research Triangle Park, NC – public television
WLTR 90.1 NPR Greenville – public radio
WCCP 105.5 – Clemson Athletics radio
WORD 106.3 – Conservative talk radio

Getting Around & Roads to Know

There's no way around it—it's hard to drive in Greenville unless you have a trustworthy GPS. It's going to take some practice, and perhaps even some good old-fashioned map studying to understand the roads here, particularly if you're used to a city on a grid. Beyond downtown, there is no grid, just a series of spokes named for the town where each eventually arrives. Also be aware that numbers are always consistent, but names can and do change…often.

146

Commit to learning the important roads and you'll save yourself a LOT of aggravation. Getting frustrated while driving is normal in any city—go easy on yourself…and study this chart!

Must-Know Roads

Roads to Know
I-85 - stretches SW to Atlanta, GA and NE to Charlotte, NC
I-385 - goes SE from downtown to I-85, then on to I-26 and Columbia, SC
123 / Academy - goes to Easley and Clemson from downtown
276 / Laurens Rd - on S side of city; aka Poinsett Hwy on N side
291 / Pleasantburg - exit 46 from I-85. Shopping and Greenville Tech
25 / White Horse - goes to T.R. then on to Hendersonville and Asheville, NC
29 / Church St / Wade Hampton - bypasses downtown, goes to Taylors, Greer
Augusta Rd - n'hood shopping, dining, connects downtown to I-85
Church St / Mills Ave - city overpass; goes S to Anderson; see also 29, above
E. North - feeder into downtown; becomes Old Spartanburg then Brushy Creek
Faris Rd - E/W artery to Pleasantburg, Augusta, 25; medical corridor
Grove Rd / Hwy 20 - links N. Augusta Rd to I-85 and Piedmont; medical corridor
Haywood Rd - 385 exit; chain restaurants; shopping; xmas trees; Haywood Mall
Laurens Rd / 276 - links T.R. to Mauldin, Simpsonville, Fountain Inn
Main St - heart of Greenville; south end goes to Augusta; north end is homes
Mauldin Rd / Butler Rd - links S. Pleasantburg to Mauldin; crosses I-385;
Millennium Blvd / Carolina Pt Pkwy - connects Laurens to Woodruff; CU-ICAR
Miller Rd / Garlington - connects Pelham to Woodruff to Laurens
Pelham Rd - links Pleasantburg to Eastside; dining & shopping; Michelin HQ
Pete Hollis / 183 - links transitional mill areas to downtown; goes W to Pickens
Pleasantburg / 291 - circles downtown to the E; crosses 385; Greenville Tech
Poinsett Hwy / 276 - from downtown to Furman, T.R. and on to 25N
Roper Mtn Rd - residential; connects Eastside to Laurens; becomes Verdae
Stone Ave - connects 385 & Laurens, to Poinsett Hwy; boutiques, salons
Verdae - connects Laurens to Woodruff; near 385 becomes Roper Mtn Rd
Washington - runs E & W from Main St, connects to Laurens at I-385 ramp
Wade Hampton / 29 - major shopping artery from downtown to Greer, Taylors
White Horse Rd / 25 - exit 44B from 85; comm/industr artery to Furman and T.R.
Woodruff Rd / 146 - shopping/big box artery; very busy exit from 385 and 85

147

Important Roads in Nearby Areas
11 - Scenic foothills road N of the city, paralleling the NC state line; leads to lakes
14 - connects Greer to Simpsonville E of Greenville; runs past GSP airport
26 - Interstate E of Greenville, connecting Asheville to Columbia and Charleston
101 - crosses I-85; runs through Greer and Taylors NE of the city, on to Hwy 11
185 - toll road that loops south of I-85; links Mills Ave to Simpsonville
290 - links northern reaches of Greenville County to Greer and Taylors

Helpful Numbers & URLs

Government Depts	Phone	Website
City of Greenville	864-232-2273	greenvillesc.gov
DMV	864-241-1145	local.dmv.org
Greenville Rec (County)	864-288-6470	greenvillerec.com
Greenville County Health Dept	864-372-3270	greenvillecountry.org
Marriage Licenses	864-467-7571	greenvillecountry.org
Greenville County School Board	864-355-3100	greenville.k12.sc.us
Greenville Police	864-467-5333	police.greenvillesc.gov
Greenville Tax Assessor	864-467-7300	greenvillecounty.org
Social Security, Greenville	864-274-5423	ssa.gov
Vehicle Tags & Licenses	864-241-1145	scdmvonline.com
Veterans Affairs	864-467-7230	greenvillecounty.org
Voter Registration	864-467-7250	scvotes.org

Greenville Cares is a one-stop service center for citizens needing information about **City programs, services and events**. Call Mon-Fri between 8 and 5.
cares@greenvillesc.gov • 864-232-2273 • greenvillesc.gov

Greenville County processes all city and county property taxes, marriage licenses and all other county-related services.
atyourservice@greenvillecounty.org • 864-467-7100 • greenvillecounty.org

SC Dept. of Transportation (DOT): 855-467-2368 • scdot.org
SC Parks, Rec, Tourism: discoversouthcaroilna.com

148

Hospitals	Phone	Website
Medical Emergency	911	
Bon Secours St. Francis Health	864-255-1000	stfrancishealth.org
Greenville Health System	864-455-7000	ghs.org
Greer Memorial Hospital	864-967-6100	ghs.org
Pelham Medical Center	864-560-6000	spartanburgregional.com
St. Francis Eastside	864-675-4000	stfrancishealth.org
Shriners Hospital for Children	864-271-3444	shrinershospitalsforchildren.org

Utilities	Phone	Website
AT&T	800-331-0500	att.com
Blue Ridge Electric Coop	800-240-3400	blueridge.coop
Broad River Electric Coop	866-687-2667	broadriverelectric.com
Charter Communications	877-207-1540	charter.com
Duke Energy	800-777-9898	duke-energy.com
Fort Hill Natural Gas Authority	864-859-6375	fhnga.com
Fountain Inn Natural Gas	864-862-0042	fountaininngas.com
Greenville Water	864-241-6000	greenvillewater.com
Greer Commission Public Works	864-848-5500	greercpw.com
Laurens Electric Coop	800-942-3141	laurenselectric.com
Little River Electric Coop	864-366-2141	lreci.coop
Piedmont Natural Gas	800-752-7504	piedmontng.com
Sprint	888-211-4727	sprint.com
T-Mobile	864-907-9855	t-mobile.com
Verizon	864-627-3000	verizon.com

Transportation	Phone	Website
Greenville Amtrak	864-255-4221	amtrak.com
Greenville Trolley	864-298-2767	greenvillesc.gov
Thurs-Fri, 6-11; Sat 10am-11pm; Sun 1-8		
GSP Airport	864-877-7426	gspairport.com
Greenlink bus system	864-467-5001	greenvillesc.gov
Taxi	864-233-6666	yellowcabgreenville.com

Organizations to Know, Find or Follow	Phone	Website
Greenville Forward	864-233-8443	greenvilleforward.com
Greenville Relocation Concierge	864-704-2409	greenvillerelocation.com
Make Greenville Yours	864-363-8628	makegreenvilleyours.com
Meetup.com/Greenville		meetup.com
Upstate International	864-631-2188	internationalupstate.org
Upstate SC Alliance	864-283-2300	upstatescalliance.com
Visit Greenville SC	800-717-0023	visitgreenvillesc.com

Business & Economic Development	Phone	Website
GADC	864-235-2008	greenvilleeconomicdevelopment.com
City's Economic Development Team	864-467-4401	greenvillesc.gov
Chamber of Commerce	864-242-1050	greenvillechamber.org
NEXT	864-990-5851	NEXTsc.org

Entertainment & Event Venues	Phone	Website
Bon Secours Arena	864-241-3800	bonsecoursarena.com
Cafe & Then Some	864-232-2287	cafeats.com
Centre Stage theater	864-233-6733	centrestage.com
Greenville Drive schedule		milb.com
Greenville Little Theatre	864-233-6238	greenvillelittletheatre.com
Greenville Parks & Rec	864-288-6470	greenvillerec.com
Greenville Zoo	864-467-4300	greenvillezoo.com
Charter Amphitheatre		charterspectrumamphitheatre.com
Peace Center	864-467-3000	peacecenter.org
SC Governor's School	864-282-3777	scgsah.org
Swamp Rabbits hockey		swamprabbits.com
TD Stage	864-467-3000	peacecenter.org
Timmons Arena	864-294-3267	timmonsarena.com
Warehouse Theater	864-235-6948	warehousetheater.com

Several local establishments offer live music: check Fete Greenville.

150

Entertainment Ideas - *Regional*	Website
Asheville Civic Center	uscellularcenterasheville.com
Asheville events	exploreasheville.com
Blue Ridge Weekends	blueridgeweekends.com
Brevard & Transylvania County, NC	visitwaterfalls.com
Brooks Center for the Performing Arts	clemson.edu/brooks
Cashiers NC events	cashiersnorthcarolina.org
Charlotte NC events	CharlottesGotALot.com
Flat Rock Cinema	flatrockcinema.com
Flat Rock Playhouse	flatrockplayhouse.org
Helen, GA events	helenga.org
Hendersonville NC events	historichendersonville.org
Highlands NC events	highlandschamber.org
Lake Lure events	aroundlakelure.com
Orange Peel, Asheville	theorangepeel.net
Mill Town Players, Pelzer	milltownplayers.org
Saluda NC events	saluda.com/events
Southern Highroads Trail events	southernhighroads.org
The Biltmore Estate	biltmore.com
Time Warner Theater, Charlotte	timewarnercablearena.com
Tryon Equestrian Center	tryon.coth.com
U.S. Cellular Center, Asheville	uscellularcenterasheville.com
Western NC events (various areas)	eventsinwnc.com

Community Center	Phone	Website
KROC Center	864-527-5948	www.krocgreenville.org

Festivals & Events	Website
All	visitgreenvillesc.com
Euphoria	euphoriagreenville.com
Artisphere	artisphere.org
Fall for GVL	fallforgreenville.net
Greek Festival	stgeorgegreenville.org
Gallabrae	gallabrae.com
Living Gallery	livinggallery.bju.edu

151

Education - Schools	Phone	Website
Greenville County	864-355-3100	greenville.k12.sc.us
Pickens County	864-397-1000	pickens.k12.sc.us
Anderson County	864-235-8768	anderson1.k12.sc.us

Education - Continuing	Phone	Website
Furman University	864-294-2000	furman.edu/sites/OLLI

Education - Higher	Website
Bob Jones University	bju.edu
Clemson University	clemson.edu
Furman University	furman.edu
Greenville Tech	gvltec.edu
University Center	ucgreenville.org
USC Med School	greenvillemed.sc.edu

Library	Phone	Website
Greenville Library	864-242-5000	greenvillelibrary.org

Local Attractions	Phone	Website
BMW Factory	1-888-Tour-BMW	bmwusfactory.com
Greenville Zoo	864-467-4300	greenvillezoo.com
Roper Mountain Science Center	864-355-8900	ropermountain.org
The Children's Museum of the Upstate	864-233-7755	tcmupstate.org
Upcountry History Museum	864-467-3100	upcountryhistory.org

Parks	Website
City of Greenville, SC	greenvillesc.gov
Parks & Trails	greenvillesc.gov/170/Parks-Trails
Greenville County Rec	greenvillerec.com

Real Estate	Website
Greater Greenville Association of Realtors	ggar.com
Greenville County Geographic Information Systems	gcgis.org

Visual Arts	Website
Bob Jones University Museum & Gallery	bjumg.org
Greenville County Museum of Art	gcma.org
Greenville Open Studios	greenvilleopenstudios.com
Metropolitan Arts Council (MAC)	greenvillearts.com

My Notes

Acknowledgments

A project like this could never be done alone—it was a massive collaboration and I have many people to thank. First of all, heartfelt gratitude to Mayor Knox White, who quickly made me fall in love with his city and who has been such a great friend, sharing his family, his knowledge and his inspiring passion for Greenville. A big thank you, also, to Bett White, Mary Ellen Wilkerson and Molly Moon, for their welcoming spirit and generosity.

There are not enough words to thank Joe Henson (aka D.J. Henson), my cheery and invaluable husband and 49-year resident, who helped with research, proofreading, photography, chart-making and shoulder rubs. I also couldn't have done this project without the help of Nancy Whitworth; Derek Lewis; my mom Johanna Boren; and author Ad Hudler, my talented and hilarious friend who generously contributed time and attention after completing his latest novel.

Additional gratitude goes out to the inspiring and hospitable VisitGreenvilleSC for its help and resources; Mike Cruice of Make Greenville Yours; the Greenville Chamber of Commerce; the City of Greenville; the GADC; Greenville Rec; The Greenville Historical Society; Greenville County School District; David Watkins Design; Lib Ramos of Indie Craft Parade; beer expert Mike Okupinski, who goes above and beyond; Alan Ethridge of the Metropolitan Arts Council; Bonnie Wallin and The Greenville Humane Society; The Kroc Tennis Center; outdoor adventure expert Jay Ferguson; the good folks at Euphoria, Artisphere, Upstate International and The Peace Center; the unparalleled and indefatigable Bob Howard; Greenville Technical College; restaurateur Carl Sobocinski; food writer M. Linda Lee; Newt Barrett; Travis Seward; Mike McCuen; style writers Ruta Fox and Taryn Scher; Warren Rollins; Julie Karrer; Crimora Carter; Dana Spinks; Marsha White; Belinda Rubio; Andrew White; Susie White; Sidney Thompson; Stacey Krall; Fredrick Dean of JusDean; RJ and Andreana Horowitz Snyder; Larry and Sandra Freeman; Lindsie Sink; Carolyn Rogers; Dance Arts Greenville; First Presbyterian Church Greenville; The Gorge; the SC Master Gardener Program; author Marian White; photo editor Lydia Schrandt; and Carrie Moloney of Evolution Design House.

–Libby McMillan Henson

154

About the Author

Libby McMillan Henson is a longtime writer, editor and producer. Prior to her 2010 move to Greenville, McMillan Henson owned a Sanibel Island destination marketing firm. She also produced an award-winning documentary for Florida public television, and contributed travel content to several regional and national magazines.

After relocating to Greenville, McMillan Henson managed digital content, 80 travel writers and social media for USA TODAY 10Best before turning her focus to this book. She still produces travel and lifestyle content for a variety of media, and her company **Greenville Relocation** eases newcomers' transitions to her city through relocation concierge services including personal assistance, custom-programmed technology and sharing of vetted resources.

When not out and about in Greenville, or on the tennis courts, Libby loves to explore Blue Ridge Mountain destinations with husband Joe, who shares her passion for travel, photography, meeting people and making fun discoveries.

	FOLLOW Libby!	**FOLLOW Libby & Joe!**
Blog + Web	greenvillerelocation.com	
Facebook	Greenville Relocation	BlueRidgeWeekends
Instagram	GreenvilleRelocation	BlueRidgeWeekends
Twitter	@GVLrelocation	
Houzz	GreenvilleRelocation	
Pinterest	GVLrelocation	

155